D0502082

YOUR MONEY OR YOUR LIFE

Why We Must Abolish the Income Tax

Sheldon Richman

ISBN 0-9640447-8-1 (hbk.) — ISBN 0-9640447-9-X (pbk.)
Copyright © 1999

The Future of Freedom Foundation
11350 Random Hills Road, Suite 800
Fairfax, Virginia 22030

Library of Congress
Catalog Card Number: 97-060308

Printed in the United States of America

Cover art by Susan Somerfield Stoffle

For Jennifer, Emily, and Benjamin

May they know the freedom of an income-tax-free world.

Contents

Acknowledgments

Many people helped me see this book through to completion. First and foremost, Jacob G. Hornberger, president of The Future of Freedom Foundation, was a unique source of moral and material support, to whom I owe a great debt. As I've said on another occasion, but for him, this book would not exist.

My friends Jeffrey Rogers Hummel and Roy E. Cordato read an early, rough manuscript and gave me excellent suggestions.

Patrick Fleenor of the Tax Foundation, Dean Stansel of the Cato Institute, David Keating and Peter Sepp of the National Taxpayers Union, and Victor Krohn of Citizens for an Alternative Tax System graciously shared data and other information.

Elaine Hawley, librarian at the Institute for Humane Studies' Harper Library, was as hospitable as any researcher could hope.

Mark Brady, formerly of IHS, and Leonard Liggio of the Atlas Economic Research Foundation helped me sort out sundry issues through provocative conversations.

Chapter 5 on the history of the income tax is based on a paper of mine written in 1990 for a Ludwig von Mises Institute conference on taxation.

Thanks, finally, to Ronald Neff for his superb copyediting and to Paige Moore for her skill at turning the manuscript into a book.

Naturally, responsibility for any errors is mine alone.

Preface

Our American ancestors created the most unusual society in history. For more than a century, Americans rejected Social Security, Medicare, Medicaid, welfare, subsidies, public schooling, trade restrictions, economic regulations, immigration controls, drug wars, and other aspects of the paternalistic welfare state that pervaded other parts of the world. This is what it once meant to be an American — to live one's life the way one chose without fear of being punished, restricted, or ordered by his government to do otherwise.

Equally important, people were free to accumulate unlimited amounts of wealth. For when they established the federal government with the Constitution in 1787, Americans deliberately refused to grant their government the power to levy taxes on their income. Throughout the nineteenth century, tens of thousands of people went from rags to riches. For the first time in history, there was absolutely nothing government officials could do about it.

The result of this unusual way of life, despite the tragic exception of slavery, was the greatest amount of freedom that man had ever seen. No one was forced to care for his neighbor. No one was punished for ingesting harmful substances. No one was compelled to send his child to school. No one was coerced into honoring his mother and father. Each person was free to make these decisions on his own.

When government had no power to take away people's income, not even to fight poverty, the result was the wealthiest society ever. And this occurred despite the massive numbers of penniless immigrants who were flooding America's shores, escaping the European lands of government guarantees against poverty to come to the land where no such guarantees existed.

But there was another unusual result. When people were free to accumulate wealth, the result was also the most charitable period that mankind had ever seen. When the Frenchman Alexis de Tocqueville visited America in the nineteenth century, he marveled at all of the voluntary charitable activities in which Americans were involved. Without being forced by government officials, Americans were voluntarily building churches, museums, opera houses, libraries, and universities.

Unfortunately, the American people of the twentieth century have abandoned the principles on which America was founded. They now embrace the way of life that people around the world have endorsed throughout history — a way of life in which government takes care of them by controlling them and their income. People in Cuba, North Korea, China, Russia, and the United States now share a joint commitment to such things as Social Security, Medicare, Medicaid, public housing, public schooling, welfare, trade and immigration controls, economic regulations and, of course, the taxes that pay for the paternalistic welfare state.

The Sixteenth Amendment to the U.S. Constitution fundamentally altered the relationship of the American citizen with his government. Prior to the amendment, it was understood that a person's income belonged to him rather than to the state. Today, the understanding is the opposite — every person's income belongs to the nation ("national income") and the government decides how much of a percentage each person shall be entitled to keep.

Moreover, Americans today have little confidence in themselves. They honestly believe that, unlike their ancestors, they must be forced by the political elite to be caring and compassionate with their friends, families, and neighbors. The thought of dismantling the socialistic welfare state, rather than simply reforming it, is terrifying to the average American.

This book is an attempt to recapture the principles on which this great nation was founded — the principles of individual liberty, private property, free markets, and freedom of choice. It is dedicated to the proposition that every individual has the inherent, inalienable right to be free, which includes the fundamental right to accumulate unlimited amounts of wealth in the marketplace and to decide what to do with that wealth. It is an attempt to encourage Americans to reflect upon and reevaluate their relationship to their government and to themselves. It is devoted to a recapturing of the self-esteem, the self-reliance, and the sense of voluntary charity that characterized our ancestors.

There are those who claim that Americans are doomed to suffer income taxation forever. But they are wrong. Ideas have consequences. They motivate people to act. If one generation could bring the Sixteenth Amendment into existence, a new generation has the power and the right to repeal it.

The twentieth century has been the century of socialism and the welfare state. Unfortunately, despite all of the misery that this dysfunctional way of life has caused, people around the world cannot abandon their addiction to it. It is up to the American people to lead the world out of this socialistic, paternalistic morass.

In order to do so, Americans must do more than simply repeal the Sixteenth Amendment. In order to lead the world to freedom, Americans must also reject the paternalistic welfare-state programs and such domestic wars as the war on poverty and the war on drugs that have scarred our society for the past several decades. When that day comes — and it ultimately will — Americans will recapture their destiny and lead the world to the highest reaches of freedom ever seen by man.

—Jacob G. Hornberger
Founder and President
The Future of Freedom Foundation

Foreword

Your Money or Your Life sounds like a threat from a highway-man, but it is not; it is the perennial threat offered, through its Internal Revenue Service agents, by the United States Congress. Sheldon Richman does a yeoman's job in showing that. He shepherds the reader through the twisted history of lies and deceit that preceded and followed the passage of the Sixteenth Amendment and hence the implementation of direct taxation that the Framers of the Constitution feared so much. Most tax critics focus their criticism of our tax code on its wastefulness, complexity, and social engineering, and on the size of the government take. While their criticism has unquestionable merit, Richman rightly and adroitly focuses on the more important moral issues the income tax raises and how it stands the Constitution's Framers' vision of a just society on its head.

One does not have to do a lot of reading to reach the conclusion that the Framers saw government as the most ruthless enemy of mankind, as exemplified by this small sample of their admonitions and warnings:

> "We must bind the powers of the state with the chains of the Constitution."
> Thomas Jefferson

> "We must confine ourselves to the powers described in the Constitution, and the moment we pass it, we take an arbitrary stride towards a despotic Government."
> James Jackson of the First Congress

"All men having power ought to be distrusted to a certain degree."
    James Madison in *The Federalist*

"We still find the greedy hand of government thrusting itself into every corner and crevice of industry, and grasping at the spoil of the multitude. Invention is continually exercised to furnish new pretenses for revenue and taxation. It watches prosperity as its prey and permits none to escape without a tribute."
    Thomas Paine

"The true theory of our Constitution is surely the wisest and best ... [for] when all government ... shall be drawn to Washington as the centre of all power, it will render powerless the checks provided of one government on another, and will become as ... oppressive as the government from which we separated."
    Thomas Jefferson

"You have rights antecedent to all earthly governments; rights that cannot be repealed or restrained by human laws; rights derived from the Great Legislator of the Universe."
    John Adams

The Framers recognized that government is a necessary evil, so they sought to limit government power to its legitimate functions by enumerating the powers of Congress. That enumeration is found in Article I, Section 8 of our Constitution. They include the power to lay and collect taxes to support armies, provide and maintain a navy, declare war, establish post offices and post roads, and a few other activities. No matter how carefully one searches the Constitution, he cannot find authority for four-fifths or more of today's federal expenditures, such as crop subsidies, business bailouts, Amtrak, welfare payments, Social Security, Medicare, ad nauseam. Furthermore, the Constitution gives no grant of authority for Congress to create the departments of Education, Commerce, or Health and Human Services, the National Endowment for the Arts, or the hundreds of other federal agencies.

Virtually all of today's federal activities boil down to either taking the property that rightfully belongs to one American and giving it to another American to whom it does not belong or granting one American a special privilege denied another American. Those activities are nothing less than the immoral use of government's brutal force to commit legalized theft and plunder, hence the aptness of Richman's title, *Your Money or Your Life.*

Some might consider Richman's title to be hyperbole, but it accurately describes what is at stake. We can readily see this by asking, What is the endgame of the following scenario? Suppose an American told the U.S. Congress, "I am an emancipated adult. I wish to be left alone to tend to my own retirement needs. If I fail to do so adequately, let me either depend on charity or suffer the consequences; however, I refuse to pay into the government's Social Security retirement program." If that person refused to fork over a part of his earnings as Social Security "contributions," the IRS would fine him. If that person rightfully concluded that he has not harmed or initiated violence against another and therefore refused to pay an unjust fine, he would be threatened with property confiscation or imprisonment. Suppose he then decided to use his natural or God-given rights to defend both his physical property against confiscation and his person against aggression? More than likely, he would suffer death at the hands of the U.S. government. The moral question Americans ought to ask is whether they can produce a moral argument that justifies a citizen's being subject to death by his government when that citizen has initiated violence against no one and simply wants to privately care for his own retirement needs? I know of no standard of morality that yields an affirmative answer.

Richman does an excellent job of documenting the political struggle that produced the Sixteenth Amendment, open season on our earnings, and the level of government control over its citizens unimaginable even by kings and tyrants. But Congress was not alone in producing today's runaway government. It was aided and abetted by a corrupt and derelict U.S. Supreme Court contemptuous of our Constitution. A sample of that contempt is the landmark 1936 decision in which the Supreme Court all but nullified Article I, Section 8 of the Constitution when it ruled that the New Deal Agriculture Adjustment Act was constitutional (*U.S. v. Butler*, 297 U.S. 65, 66 [1936]). The Court wrote, "The power of Congress to authorize appropriations of public money for public purposes is not limited by the direct grants of legislative power found in the Constitution." The Court essentially told Congress that it does not matter what the Constitution says. It does not matter what limits the Constitution places on government; they have the right to do as they please and engage in whatever activities they please. The Court's decision helps to explain how the federal government came to spend more than 25 percent of our GNP, compared with the 4 percent expenditure (except during wars) from the birth of our nation to the 1920s.

The current income tax code is complicated, abusive, and invasive and is long overdue for elimination. While the nation debates this issue, it will serve us well to recognize that if the federal government seeks to collect $1,600,000,000,000 of the people's earnings, it must establish an oppressive system of collection, whether under the current code, a flat tax, or a national sales tax.

As Sheldon Richman argues, any long-term solution to the problems and threats to liberty created by the federal government must address itself to the moral and constitutional issues associated with the activities of the U.S. Congress, the White House, and rulings of the U.S. Supreme Court.

—Walter E. Williams
John M. Olin Distinguished
Professor of Economics and
Chairman of the Economics Department
George Mason University, Fairfax, Virginia

Introduction

The singular feature of the twentieth century has been the dominance of an anticapitalist mentality. Accumulated private wealth has been considered the result of greed, exploitation, and misrepresentation. How else could some people have acquired personal riches other than at the expense of others? At the same time, significant inequalities in income and wealth have been considered unfair and immoral. What equality of opportunity can exist in society when some start out with greater financial resources with which to play in the game of life?

Through most of human history, wealth often *was* acquired through force, plunder, and exploitation. Marauding bands of cutthroats and thieves would descend upon villages and towns, looting the meager wealth and food supplies of the hapless victims. Kings and princes and bloodthirsty adventurers would conquer various regions and territories and impose their will upon the occupants of the land; tribute, compulsory labor, and onerous taxes and tithes would be demanded under threat of terror, torture, and death. Regulations, controls, and restrictions would be established over the economic activities of the poor residents of these areas by those who made themselves lords and masters over their violently acquired domains. Caste and class structures were established that guaranteed that the conquerors and their descendants were assured permanent privileges at the expense of those of lower rank who were made to work and produce for a politically protected elite.

This was the social environment in which countless generations of human beings throughout the world have worked and lived out their lives. Only during the last 300 years did this social condition begin to change, with its epicenter in a revolution of ideas in Europe and North America. Scholars, thinkers, and philosophers began to articulate a notion of the rights of man. They rejected the ancient Greek idea that some men were naturally meant to be masters while others were born to be slaves. They secularized the Christian idea that all men are equal in the eyes of God. This new notion of the rights of man reached its clearest formulation in those stirring words of the American Declaration of Independence: "We hold these Truths to be self-evident, that all Men are created equal, that they are endowed by their Creator with certain unalienable Rights, that among these are Life, Liberty, and the Pursuit of Happiness — That to secure these Rights, Governments are instituted among Men, deriving their just Powers from the Consent of the Governed."

The same year that the American Founding Fathers articulated the basis for the fundamental and universal rights of every human being, the Scottish moral philosopher Adam Smith published *The Wealth of Nations*, in which he explained the idea of a "system of natural liberty." Once all forms of government regulation, control, and privilege were done away with, the obvious and simple system of natural liberty establishes itself of its own accord. Every man, as long as he does not violate the laws of justice, is left perfectly free to pursue his own interest his own way and to bring both his industry and capital into competition with those of any other man, or order of men. The sovereign is completely discharged from a duty, in the attempting to perform which he must always be exposed to innumerable delusions, and for the proper performance of which no human wisdom or knowledge could ever be sufficient — the duty of superintending the industry of private people and of directing it towards the employments most suitable to the interest of the society.

In such a system of natural liberty, Adam Smith argued, government would be restricted to a small number of functions, the primary one being the protection of each individual's right to life and property through courts of law, police, and national defense. In essence, government was no longer to be an agency of force and compulsion for bestowing privileges and favors on some at the material and social expense of others.

The world was transformed in unimaginable ways by these ideas of political and economic liberty. Not only were men now made free through equal rights before the law; they were increasingly liberated from the plundering and privilege-making powers of government. Human relationships began to be based on mutual agreement and voluntary association. The free-market society replaced the servile state of the feudal order and the mercantilist system of regulation.

The free market's social system of division of labor is one of mutual interdependency and mutual service for common benefit. Voluntary exchange means that no one can get what is the property of another without that other's willingness to part with the property he rightfully owns. Each participant in this system of division of labor, therefore, must orient himself towards the wants and desires of his fellow men if he is to succeed in offering a good or service that others will be willing to take in trade for what he would like to acquire in exchange.

As a result, in the free marketplace, each is both a servant and a master. As a producer, each of us must serve our neighbors by marketing a product others will be interested in buying; and we must try to offer it at a price at least as competitive as our closest rivals, who also are themselves attempting to win the consumers' business. If we fail to do so, we are then limited in our own ability to reenter the market as a consumer, where those same others must now serve us so they can earn the financial wherewithal to buy from us in the next round of the never-ending network of market transactions.

Income and wealth, therefore, in the free market are not the result of plunder, privilege, or political power. They are what each of us has earned for services rendered based on what other members of the society consider our services to be worth in furthering their own plans and purposes. The successful, profit-making entrepreneurs are the ones who are better at anticipating what others might find it attractive to buy and who, being more cost-efficient producers, are able to sell at the lowest prices possible. In the division of labor, those who lack the entrepreneurial quality or who are more risk-averse in the face of the uncertainties of the business world hire out their services for market-determined wages. Each employee's income is a reflection of what an employer thinks his services are worth in the manufacture of a potentially consumer-demanded product, in competition with other would-be employers who might hire that worker for their own production activities instead. Those who earn interest incomes do so by voluntarily forgoing other uses they might have for their own wealth and lending it to others who are willing to pay a price in the future (in the form of interest) for having use of some of that wealth for enterprising endeavors they have in mind.

As the classical liberals of the nineteenth century clearly argued, the beauty of the free-market economy is that it harnesses the self-interest and productive potential of each of the society's members in the service of their fellow men. And it does so without force or command. It leaves each man free to peacefully go his own way, but to go his own way in a social setting in which the advancement of his own ends directs him towards furthering the ends of others at the same time.

The relative incomes earned by participants in the free-market economy are derived from neither exploitation nor plunder because the very principle upon which market exchanges are based — voluntary and mutually agreed-upon terms of trade — precludes the existence of unjust or unfair material gains. If some enter the market as consumers with a greater monetary capacity for buying available goods and services, it is a reflection of their greater reward in their role as producers in successfully meeting the consumer demands of their fellow men in that same market process.

But in the middle and late decades of the nineteenth century, counterrevolutionary forces arose in opposition to the revolutionary liberation of the free-market society. The most important of these counterrevolutionary forces were socialism and the interventionist-welfare state. The socialists perversely said that the worker selling his labor services for wages to an employer in the market was the same as the medieval serf compelled to work for the lord of the manor. They saw no difference between the free man who voluntarily contracts for wages in an open competitive market and the serf bound to the land and compelled to work at the lord's command under threat of physical punishment or death. In the place of the system of private property and market competition, the socialists called for the radical nationalization of all the means of production, with the state then acting as the central planner of all production and the single employer of all those needing to work to earn a living.

Many intellectuals, political philosophers, and active politicians accepted the socialist critique of capitalist society but did not want to follow the socialists in their call for the radical transformation of the social order. Instead, they advocated a redressing of the supposed abuses of free-wheeling, "unbridled" capitalism through a "middle way" of industrial regulation and redistribution of income and wealth.

In the twentieth century, these socialist and interventionist-welfare statist ideas and policies have triumphed all around the world. Even in the present "post-communist" era, the prevailing ideological and political ideas still rest on the socialist premise that a truly free-market capitalism would be harmful to the general interests of society, threatening the exploitation of many and resulting in an unjust distribution of income among the various individuals and groups.

For 150 years, the income tax has been considered a fundamental weapon in the arsenal of government powers to correct the supposed "evils" and "abuses" of capitalism. In the *Communist Manifesto*, published in 1848, Karl Marx and Friedrich Engels formulated their most famous condemnation of capitalist society. After articulating their reasons for believing that capitalism would eventually pass away and be replaced by the socialist society of the future, they proposed a ten-point program for "despotic inroads on the rights of property ... as a means of entirely revolutionizing the mode of production." The second point in their program called for "a heavy progressive or graduated income tax." If a violent transformation of the social order could not be implemented at one stroke, then at least the wealth of the rich could be cut down and slowly eroded over time through a progressive income tax.

Even when the income tax has not been thought of as a conscious tool for bringing about the complete end to the capitalist order, it has been considered a useful and indispensable method for manipulating social outcomes and redistributing wealth into more desired patterns. As one example, James E. Meade, who received the Nobel Prize in economics in 1977, published a book entitled *Planning and the Price Mechanism* in 1948 (just one hundred years after the *Communist Manifesto*) in which he proposed what he called "the liberal-socialist solution" to social problems. He said that those who "labored to obtain a more equal distribution of income and property may well be proud of their achievements which ... have brought about a quiet but complete social revolution in the last ten years" through an increasingly more progressive income tax.

The income tax, in Meade's view, was one of the useful and necessary "radical measures to ensure a tolerably equitable distribution of income and property." His only fear was that if the income tax was pushed too high towards the 100 percent mark, it would kill the goose that laid the productive eggs by undermining incentives for work and investment. Hence, one needed to manipulate the income tax rate to achieve some "optimal" combination of income equity and productive efficiency. He was confident the social engineers of the interventionist-welfare state had the knowledge and ability to ensure that goal.

The socialists and interventionists have understood that if government can directly tax income, then the political authority has within its power the ability to control both the wealth-creating and spending processes. Like the medieval lord of the manor, who demanded a portion of the physical output of the land produced by the serfs and thus determined how much of the sustenance of life would be left in the hands of those who had produced it, the advocates of the income tax have wanted to control how much of what each of us has earned in the marketplace shall be left in our respective hands. They have wanted to be the political lords and masters who determine how much we each have to live on and how the remainder that is taxed away shall be spent and redistributed to fulfill their collectivist fantasies.

The difference between 1948 and now is that in the immediate post–World War II era, the socialists and interventionists of the day were filled with ideological confidence that they could set the world on to a better and brighter utopian future through their wise leadership and technical expertise as economists and statisticians. Today, the interventionist-welfare states of Europe and the United States have almost no ideological purpose other than serving and pandering to the ocean of special-interest groups who each want to manipulate the tax codes and the income-tax schedules to serve their narrow designs at the expense of the rest of the society. In this sense, the income tax has lost its collectivist ideological rationale; lip service is still paid to "social justice" and "income fairness," but everyone knows that these are merely covers for plunder, privilege, and income transfers for those interest groups at the expense of the society as a whole.

In the immediate aftermath of the First World War, economist Joseph Schumpeter published an essay entitled "The Crisis of the Tax State." He argued that there is no better way to understand the social forces at work in a society than to investigate that society's fiscal history, because in the taxing and spending policies of government are to be seen everything that is important for understanding how and why entire peoples and cultures have declined and decayed throughout the ages.

In the pages of the book you hold in your hand, Sheldon Richman has unmasked the reality of the American tax state. With logical eloquence and detailed historical accuracy, he demonstrates the immorality, injustice, corruption, and inefficiency of America's income tax system. No one who reads this book can ever again see the income tax as anything other than the dragon seed of evil that is eating away at the moral and productive fiber of American society. After explaining why the income tax must be abolished if a free America is to be restored, Mr. Richman forcefully reminds us that taxes are only one side of the fiscal coin. Governments tax so much because they spend so much. And governments spend so much because of all that an increasing number of us lobby government to do for us. The monster tax state will be successfully slain only when we have also defeated the monster spending state.

For almost ten years, The Future of Freedom Foundation has devoted its activities to unmasking, criticizing, and defeating the socialist and the interventionist-welfare statist ideas of our time. Mr. Richman's book is an important contribution to this effort. It has been said that the power to tax is the power to destroy. Since the passage of the Sixteenth Amendment to the Constitution in 1913, the U.S. government has had one of the most destructive of those taxing powers in its hands. It is time to take it away. It is time to deny government the right to intrude into our lives and investigate how we earn and spend our income, while at the same time intimidating tens of millions of people into becoming obedient tax slaves through the threat of confiscation and imprisonment. The future of freedom depends upon our total victory over this monster taxing and spending state.

— *Richard M. Ebeling*
Vice-President of Academic Affairs
The Future of Freedom Foundation

1

The Permanent War

About ten years ago Stanley McGill, 93, mailed a check for $7,000 to the Internal Revenue Service. When he died, his daughter discovered that Mr. McGill had made a mistake. The money should not have been sent. Marian Brockamp explained to the IRS that her father was senile and asked for a refund.

The IRS said no. Requests for refunds must be made within three years.

Mrs. Brockamp took the case to court. It went all the way to the U.S. Supreme Court.

She lost.[1]

In the grand scheme of things, that is a small event. The Internal Revenue Service has done far worse in its time. It has harassed and tormented people. It has seized property and frozen bank accounts. It has ruined credit records. It has driven people to suicide. Nevertheless, the Stanley McGill story sums up a great deal about the IRS and the American tax system. The IRS concedes that the $7,000 should not have been sent. It is money that the agency should never have received. Mr. McGill made a mistake. His daughter informed the IRS as soon as she discovered the error. No one questions the facts. But the IRS won't surrender the money. And now the U.S. Supreme Court says the IRS doesn't have to. (The Ninth Circuit Court had ruled that it was "unconscionable" for the government to keep the money.)

Speaking for a unanimous court, Justice Stephen G. Breyer wrote:

The nature and potential magnitude of the administrative problem suggest that Congress decided to pay the price of occasional unfairness in individual cases ... to maintain a more workable tax enforcement system.

Congress decided to pay the price? How noble. Except that in this case it appears Congress has forced Mr. McGill's heirs to pay the price. Why? Because the rights of the individual must not be permitted to create administrative problems for the IRS or to interfere with the maintenance of a workable tax enforcement system.

Yes, that incident occurred in the United States of America.

Imagine if the tables were turned and after Mr. McGill's death the IRS discovered that he "owed" the government $7,000. Imagine further that Mrs. Brockamp politely replied that the IRS was too late in its request. What would have happened? The IRS would have seized the money and perhaps have made hell out of Mrs. Brockamp's life. And the Supreme Court would have sided with the IRS.[2]

The IRS reign of terror is something we have unfortunately grown accustomed to. But someday it might be different. Someday we will look back on the era of the income tax and the IRS with embarrassment that such an immoral system could exist in this noble land. We will be bewildered that this system could have been adopted in 1913, considering the revolutionary libertarian roots of the great American experiment in freedom. How could the American people have permitted and put up with the Internal Revenue Service, which tax historian Charles Adams equates with "a miniature Soviet state with the power to intimidate just about everyone"?[3]

This book tries to put the income tax, and the Sixteenth Amendment that permitted it, into historical context and show its implications for morality, the relationship between citizen and state, and the quest for prosperity. The verdict on the tax is not favorable: ratification of the amendment and passage of the tax was a major turning point in the transmogrification of America from republic to democratic despotism. More than anything else, it converted Americans from citizens to subjects. Indeed, there is not a single good thing that can be said about the income tax.

In fiscal year 1997, the federal government spent about $1.6 trillion. Income taxation in one form or another raised about $1.3 trillion. One trillion, three hundred billion dollars. Think about that. Americans are paying between 15 percent and more than 30 percent of their adjusted gross income, thousands of dollars a year for the working and middle classes, in personal income taxes alone.

They pay more than 15 percent for Social Security and Medicare. In hidden ways they pay the corporate income tax. According to the Tax Foundation, the personal income tax takes almost 10 percent of net national product. Do Americans get their money's worth? The question answers itself. As Will Rogers said, thank goodness we don't get all the government we pay for.

But even to ask about getting one's money's worth is to miss the point. The tax system and the distributive engine it fuels are not about giving citizens value for value. Only voluntary exchange can accomplish that. The IRS may call the taxpayers "customers," but the point of the system is to milk them to the maximum without setting off a revolt and to use the money to keep politicians and bureaucrats in power. As that great tax collector Jean-Baptiste Colbert, Louis XIV's controller general, said, "The art of taxation consists in so plucking the goose as to get the most feathers with the least hissing."

In carrying out its mission, the IRS is only serving a higher power: the lawmakers who need a never-ending flow of cash to the federal treasury. They wrote the laws that loosed the IRS on the American people. They can repeal them. Why don't they? They want the money, pure and simple.

Nuclear-Proof Taxation

To see the government's true priorities, consider that when the threat of nuclear war with the Soviet Union loomed, a top government concern was how to collect taxes after 100 million Americans were killed and U.S. society was devastated. A Department of Treasury document on the subject was titled "Fiscal Planning for Chaos." A later memorandum noted that the tax system would vary from place to place, depending on the amount of destruction. Where damage was cataclysmic, martial law would be declared and government officials would simply seize whatever resources they needed. "Simply stated," according to the memo, "everybody would be in the Army."[5]

But officials anticipated that a market economy, with money, would spontaneously return (a perceptive observation, for that is what would happen). Because of that, the government would have to be ready with a tax system. At first a flat-rate gross-receipts tax would be adequate. Since the range of post-attack incomes would be small, the memo said, the income tax as we know it would not be necessary. But the income tax would be waiting in the wings. As the memo put it:

3

Nevertheless, it would be desirable to have on the books a personal income tax at the outset of the emergency. The reasons for the very early establishment of a personal income tax, even though the private economic sector may have ceased to function, are that (1) the Revenue Service should have time to plan the administration of the tax ... and (2) liability should be established at the earliest phases of the emergency *to tax illegal gains made by speculators and black market operators* [emphasis added].[6]

Hold on a minute. Illegal gains? Speculators? Black-market operators? What was the treasury secretary talking about? When people begin to trade after a nuclear war, what would count as an illegal gain? Presumably the government would control prices, and anyone charging a higher price would be guilty of making an illegal gain. Who would be a speculator — anyone who buys low and sells high? What does "black market" mean in this context? Typically, a black market is the underground trade in illegal products. The Treasury memo implies that any trade that is not authorized or monitored by the government would be illegal. Dazed Americans would be trying to rebuild their lives, but the national government would be busy controlling economic activity and making sure taxes were collected.

A later Treasury study recommended a 24 percent general retail sales tax in lieu of an income tax if IRS records are destroyed. Interestingly, the study stated that the sales tax would encourage savings and allow the rebuilding of the capital stock. (The growing movement to replace the income tax with a national retail sales tax makes exactly that argument.)

The government's chief worry about nuclear war was that in the chaos, the American people would go untaxed. If the government were cut off from the money, how would it maintain its operations? What if people discovered they can get along without the bloated national state we labor under today?

For David Burnham, author of *A Law Unto Itself: Power, Politics and the IRS*, this concern with collecting taxes after nuclear devastation validates Benjamin Franklin's famous maxim that nothing is certain but death and taxes. As Burnham puts it, "In a most concrete way, the unswerving determination of these officials to complete their mission no matter how desperate the nation's condition confirms the wisdom of the death-and-taxes observation of the sage of Philadelphia."[7]

Who is surprised to learn that government officials regard protection of the revenue flow as a key consideration when planning for nuclear war? They are the same people who raise estate taxes retroactively, upsetting the plans made by people before they died. What better indicates the true relationship between the citizen and the state?

The Income Tax under Attack

Today we hear more criticism of the income tax and the IRS than ever before. The chairman of the House Ways and Means Committee, Rep. Bill Archer of Texas, has called for abolition of the tax and the IRS (and its replacement with a national retail sales tax). Sen. Richard Lugar made repeal of the income tax a pillar of his short-lived presidential bid. Presidential candidate Robert Dole promised to end the IRS "as we know it." Whether they would actually rid America of the IRS is beside the point. They thought it was worth telling the American people that there is something gravely wrong with the income-tax system. They targeted the IRS and its reviled practices. That is progress.

Of course, we've heard this before. President Jimmy Carter called the tax code a disgrace. President Ronald Reagan said something similar and oversaw so-called tax-reform legislation. Changes were made, rates were cut (then raised by his successors), the code was simplified in places (before being made more complicated again), and brackets were indexed for inflation. But overall, it's the same old tax code. Meanwhile, the other income tax, the payroll tax that supports Social Security and part of Medicare, was raised for several years running. Tax reform has become one of the biggest scams in America. No wonder no one got excited when Robert Dole tried to make it the centerpiece of his presidential campaign.

This book has essentially one theme: taxation of income is bad. All taxation involves coercion and thus violates individual rights. If you don't believe that, ask yourself why there are penalties, including imprisonment, for nonpayment and failure to file a return, that is, report to the government on your financial activities. Libertarians believe taxation is theft. That matter will be taken up in detail in the next chapter. For now, let's leave it at this: when you take someone's money without his consent, it is stealing. It doesn't matter that the majority of the victim's fellow citizens voted for it. It is theft and nothing but theft. The nineteenth-century political philosopher and constitutional lawyer Lysander Spooner said he could see no difference between the government and a highwayman. Actually, he could find one difference: the highwayman does not hector his victim, insisting that the thievery was good for him.

But this is not a general book about taxation. As bad as any taxation is, the income tax is worse. It is aggravated theft, robbery with malice aforethought. Theoretically, all forms of taxation could be draconian. If a sales tax caused mass evasion through the cash economy, the government could conceivably conduct house-to-house searches demanding receipts for all the products you own. If a revenue tariff were sufficiently evaded, one can imagine the government torturing consumers to get them to identify the smugglers. The late economist Murray Rothbard was right when he insisted that ultimately what counts is how much the government transfers from the productive sector to the parasitic sector, not how it does so.

That said, it is nevertheless the case that in practice the income tax has been more abusive of the people's rights than other taxes. It lends itself more readily to draconian enforcement. That justifies singling it out for special condemnation. But we should not forget that merely replacing the income tax with another tax designed to raise the same revenue would be a shallow victory.[8]

The moment the principle of income taxation is granted, the ground is prepared for myriad abuses of the people. As will be elaborated in the pages to follow, if the government is permitted to tax incomes, it will demand reams of personal information about each citizen's financial endeavors. It will compel people to report on the peaceful financial activities of other people. But more than that, it must have the muscle to check that information, to spy on people, to conduct inquisitions, and to punish — hard. Why? Because there is nothing more natural than people's trying to keep what they worked to acquire. Regardless of their explicit political philosophy, most people are implicit advocates of property rights. They don't like being dispossessed of their belongings. Even thieves don't like to be robbed. Despite years of indoctrination about taxes' being voluntary and the price of civilization, most people deep down realize that the tax system is seizing something dear to them — the fruits of their labor. And they don't like it. So they do what they can to minimize the damage. They use every legal means to keep their money (television and radio commercials and books constantly offer ways to reduce one's tax liability), and they sometimes use illegal ways. The distinction is not always clear. The IRS says collections fall short of what is "due" by about $150 billion a year.

That is the total of contested claims; it does not include taxes on incalculable income made in the underground economy, estimated at 20 to 50 percent of GDP.[9]

Man vs. State

Income taxation inaugurates a permanent war between the people, who want to keep what they earn, and the government, which wants as much of it as it can get. The government tries to make the war less obvious by deadening the pain when possible. The withholding tax makes it unnecessary for most Americans to write checks to the IRS; indeed, they eagerly await their refunds. But the war is part of the American psyche nonetheless. All Americans sense that an awesome power lurks, ready to grab an increasing portion of anything they earn. That adversary relationship has far-reaching consequences for a society founded on the principles of the Declaration of Independence, namely, the rights to life, liberty, and the pursuit of happiness. In the Declaration, Thomas Jefferson said that when government fails to protect rights or itself threatens them, the people have the right and duty to "alter or abolish" it.[10] That surely indicates that according to the prevailing philosophy among Americans at the time, government was the dangerous servant. The people were the master. But the income tax turns that relationship on its head. The tax and all the powers that must accompany it turn the people into cowering servants, ever fearful of being accused of concealing income or information and being compelled to prove otherwise. People have lost money, homes, businesses, and liberty to the IRS. A few have committed suicide under the pressure of a tax investigation. The income tax may not be the root of *all* evil, as the libertarian writer Frank Chodorov believed. But it is the root of many evils. The income tax radically undermined the American revolution.

Every American should ask himself what it was like to live in the United States before there was an income tax. Imagine not having to give up more than 30 percent of your income to the federal government. Imagine living without fear of being audited by the IRS. Imagine starting the new year and not having to think about where you stored the previous year's receipts. Imagine not worrying whether your records are good enough for the IRS. Imagine not having to pay a tax preparer hundreds of dollars to fill out complicated forms in order to minimize your tax liability and avoid audit. Imagine such a world in which none of those burdens existed.

Americans lived without those fears and burdens for more

than one hundred years (except in the Civil War era). They built a decent society nonetheless. Late-nineteenth-century America was the freest society in history. People could run their own lives with little interference from government. Prosperity increased as never before. Products that once only the nobility could afford became mass consumer goods. Specialization and the division of labor increased productivity, which in turn raised living standards. Taxes, mostly excise taxes and revenue tariffs, took only a small portion of people's wealth. The federal government played only a bit part in the lives of the people. (That role was enlarged by the Civil War but was still small by later standards.[11])

The government does not publish figures for how much of GDP the national government absorbed in the late nineteenth century. But it does have them going back to 1930. In that year, before the income tax affected ordinary people, federal receipts were just 4.2 percent of GDP. (Spending accounted for an even smaller part, 3.4 percent.) In 1942, the share of GDP extracted by the federal government hit double digits for the first time, exceeding 10 percent. It essentially has gone up ever since. Today it stands at more than 21 percent, the highest since World War II.

The income tax has been a key factor in the growth of government. When enacted, only the few richest people in America paid the tax. In 1934 individual income taxes provided about 14 percent of federal receipts. It became a tax for ordinary people during World War II, ironically under that reputed champion of ordinary people, Franklin Delano Roosevelt. Today, it accounts for more than 43 percent. Payroll taxes for Social Security and Medicare account for about 35 percent. As you can see, Americans' incomes have provided a rich vein for the government to mine. The income tax makes it easy for the government to raise money. Its sheer complexity often makes it difficult for people to know what any given change in the tax code will mean for their own situations. By the time they realize that their taxes have gone up, it is too late.

An ugly picture emerges. As we will see, the income tax has:

- Given the government unprecedented access to the American people's wealth.
- Provided the rationale for the government to intrude into our personal affairs.
- Reversed the traditional rule-of-law relationship between government and those suspected of lawbreaking.
- Corrupted morality by labeling efforts to keep one's own money as "cheating."

- Bewildered the American people with constantly changing technical rules that no one could possibly comply with perfectly.
- Permitted lawmakers to influence our conduct through selective tax deductions and exemptions.

All this has come from the principle that government may tax incomes. As objectionable as other taxes are, none could permit the government to amass power, abuse citizens, or corrupt society the way the income tax has. That is why repealing the tax, along with the Sixteenth Amendment that permits it, is an essential blow in the struggle against power and for liberty.

This book will not be comforting to those who love freedom. It will show that the tax system is offensive to morality and destructive of civil liberties and prosperity. We will retrace the fateful steps America took on its way to adopting the income tax. If a sense of incredulity — even horror — overtakes readers it will be unsurprising. Looking back, it is hard to believe that a country conceived in liberty could have taken the path it did and permitted the federal government to exercise such awesome power.

If at the end readers come to the conclusion that the income tax was a tragic decision in the history of America, if they come to believe that life would be better for everyone without that tax, if they understand that liberty is worth more than anything the income tax finances, and if they resolve to help rid America of that tyranny — then this book will have succeeded in its mission.

Let's begin the journey to freedom.

Notes

[1] Joan Biskupic, "IRS Is Resting Place of Dead Man's Error," *Washington Post*, February 19, 1997, A6.

[2] On paper the IRS faces a statute of limitations. But as we will see in chapter 3, the agency has ways to get around that restriction.

[3] Charles Adams, *For Good and Evil: The Impact of Taxes on the Course of Civilization* (Lanham, Md.: Madison Books, 1993), p. 385.

[4] For details see David Burnham, *A Law Unto Itself: Power, Politics and the IRS* (New York: Random House, 1989), pp. 3–6.

[5] Quoted from a 1967 memo from Treasury Secretary Henry H. Fowler to Price Daniel, director of the Office of Emergency Planning, in ibid., p. 4.

[6] Quoted in ibid., p. 5.

[7] Ibid., p. 6.

[8] Thanks to Jeffrey Rogers Hummel for contributing to my understanding of this matter.

[9] This information was furnished by Patrick Fleenor at the Tax Foundation.

[10] Curiously, on the wall of the Jefferson Memorial where portions of the Declaration are reproduced, the reference to the right of revolution is left out. The memorial was built during the Franklin Roosevelt years.

[11] For details on how the Civil War changed the American republic, see Jeffrey Rogers Hummel, *Emancipating Slaves, Enslaving Free Men: A History of the American Civil War* (Chicago: Open Court, 1996).

2

The Immorality of the Income Tax

P roponents of the income tax have some explaining to do. By what right does the government take a portion of each person's income without his consent before he even gets his hands on it? By what right does the government require each citizen to furnish highly personal information about the sources and amount of money he makes each year? By what right does the government threaten fines, property seizure, and imprisonment if it deems that information false and is unsatisfied with a citizen's response?

The income tax has become such an accepted part of life that most people never think to ask those questions. But those questions — and the income tax itself — should stick in the craw of a society that prides itself on being free. There was a time when it did just that. At an earlier period in American history, when the glow of the memory of the American Revolution shined far brighter that it does today, citizens of the United States were repelled by the thought of having their earnings taxed. They thought it was unseemly for the government to make inquiries into such private matters as one's income-producing activities and then to take even a small percentage of it. (The word "inquisitorial" was often used to describe such a tax.) Adam Smith, whom the Founders admired, wrote, "By subjecting the people to frequent visits and odious examination of the tax gatherers, [the government] may expose them to much unnecessary trouble, vexation and oppression."[1]

In our time, one of the few men to shine the light of morality

11

on the income tax was the great libertarian writer Frank Chodorov. His little classic, *The Income Tax: The Root of All Evil*,[2] remains an unanswered indictment of the very principle of income taxation. In it Chodorov pointed out that America was based on the principle of man's natural rights and that "any political action which attempts to violate these rights violates his human-ness, and thus becomes 'evil.'" He sought to trace the many evils committed by the U.S. government to the power granted in the Sixteenth Amendment. "That is the 'root,'" he wrote.[3]

Chodorov recognized how drastically the amendment altered the nature of the national government. Rather than a protector of rights, he said, "it is fast becoming a government that conceives of itself to be the source of rights.... In short, America is no longer the America of the Declaration of Independence."[4]

Taxation Is Theft

Before we discuss the morality of income taxation in detail, we should consider taxation per se. All forms of taxation have an essential characteristic in common. Taxation is the government's commandeering of money from its citizens. The state compels people to surrender that sum under threat of fine or imprisonment if they fail to do so. It takes something that belongs to someone else. At the most intuitive level, that is unjust. That power is unique to government. Where others can only ask payment (and withhold goods and services if it is not forthcoming), the state can demand it no matter what the taxpayers' wishes are. Regardless of the kind of tax, the state says: "Pay or else — no questions asked." The amount surrendered may be computed on the price of a product bought (the sales tax), or on the value of real estate (the property tax), or on annual wages and salaries (the income tax). The central fact remains: the state demands a sum of money, and refusal is punishable. Coercion is what makes taxation immoral.

The nineteenth-century English libertarian Auberon Herbert wrote that "the first and greatest question [about taxation] is whether to help oneself to one's neighbor's property by force is or is not morally right."[5]

So much for the U.S. government's favorite claim that the income tax is voluntary. A tax is about as voluntary as conscription. As Rep. Charles Rangel of New York, a Democratic member of the House Ways and Means Committee, said, apparently without irony, "What makes a voluntary system work is the fear of sanctions and penalties."[6] Judge Learned Hand put it well: "Taxes are enforced exactions, not voluntary contributions."[7]

The coercive and unjust nature of taxation has profound implications for any discussion of the morality of government funding. As the late economist Murray Rothbard asked, how can there be canons of just taxation if it is by nature unjust? Beginning with Adam Smith, many economists have offered such canons. But Rothbard pointed out, "If taxation itself is unjust, then it is clear that no allocation of its burdens, however ingenious, can be declared just."[8] For example, it has been said that taxes should treat people in the same situation equally. The "equality" principle sounds like the epitome of fairness. But Rothbard objects: if taxation is unjust per se, the equality principle fails. There is no justice in equal injustice. He applied his objection to the common view that loopholes such as tax exemptions are unjust. Those terms indicate that something is *not* taxed. Our objection, he said, should not be that some things are not taxed; rather, it should be that everything else is! Uniformity is not just impractical; it is impossible for a variety of reasons. For example, since any tax system must rearrange income through the transfer of money, some people, such as bureaucrats and beneficiaries of government programs, will benefit more than others. That makes the tax system nonuniform.[9] Rothbard similarly undermines each of the venerable canons of tax justice by the reminder that taxation is intrinsically evil.

In moral terms, it does not matter that the government claims to render services vaguely in return for tax payments. If a mugger shines his victim's shoes before absconding with his booty, we don't change our moral judgment of him. He is still a thief. Why? Because, unlike a trader in the market, he gives his victim no choice; it's "your money or your life."

The government does the same thing. The skeptical reader might object that citizens in a democratic society *do* have a say. They have the right to vote for the officeholders who will decide tax policy; sometimes the people even vote on taxes directly in referendums. Aren't they in fact taxing *themselves*? There are many problems with this answer.

To begin with, many people don't vote. They may have the legal right to do so, but they opt out of the process. Why are they taxed anyway? And what of those who voted for the losing candidates? Maybe those citizens voted as they did because they disliked the tax policies of the winning candidates. Why are they taxed anyway?

The standard reply here is that once an election is held, no one has a right to complain about the outcome: Those who supported the winners got their way; those who voted for the losers knew going in that success was not guaranteed; and those who did not vote chose to leave the matter to others. As the nineteenth-century English philosopher Herbert Spencer pointed out, that argument neatly rigs the game. No one may protest the outcome of an election and the ensuing policies, however burdensome. The democratic system is conveniently immunized against complaint.

If people are taxed regardless of whether and how they vote, it can't be the case that they tax themselves. In fact, taxation undermines the very idea of a free election because the votes are cast under duress. The most we can establish is that people have some say in who will mug them. But it's a small say: the chances of being killed in an auto accident en route to the polls are greater than the chances of one vote's determining the outcome of most elections.

There are other problems with the "we tax ourselves" position. An impressive literature from the "pubic choice" school of political economy demonstrates that the people do not make tax policy, even in the sense that their representatives ascertain and carry out the people's will with respect to taxes. On the contrary, in practice the legislature acts as a clearinghouse for the bidding and lobbying of organized interest groups, which, unlike the unorganized body of citizens, have the incentive and resources to directly influence government policy for their own benefit. In other words, textbook democratic theory aside, legislators are not even trying to make tax policy in the interest of "the people." That policy, like most else that government does, is intended to transfer resources from the many to the few.[10]

One political economist who saw these issues clearly was J.-B. Say in France. Writing in the early nineteenth century, Say understood that taxation was not consented to and that it was not for the purpose of increasing the people's welfare. What does consent mean, asked Say, when the government gives the people no choice *but* to consent?[11] As to the view that taxing and spending benefit the people, Say pointed out that taxation is a burden imposed by the "ruling power" for its own purposes.[12]

We thus can dispose of the view that taxation is equivalent to a person's moving his money from one pocket to another. It is much more like being mugged by a mugger who occasionally shines his victim's shoes, although most of the time, what's left on the shoes is not Shinola.

It is also incorrect to suppose that taxes are like dues paid for

14

membership in a club. When a person joins a club, he typically acquires rights to use facilities that belong to others. Dues are the price of access to those facilities. If a person refuses to pay, he is denied membership, not arrested. Taxation obviously works differently. Someone remaining on his own property and not actively using the government's services still must pay taxes. The club analogy breaks down.

The Income Tax

Those considerations apply to any form of taxation. But this is a book about the income tax. There are moral criticisms that have special application, at least in practice, to that tax alone. Frank Chodorov pointed out that the premise of the income tax is that the government really owns everything. He wrote that it "unashamedly proclaims the doctrine of collectivized wealth.... That which it does not take is a concession."[13]

That is the single most important fact about the income tax. It is a blank check for the government. One year it can demand 50 percent of people's income at the top end. Then it can lower the rate to 28 percent. Then it can raise it to 31 percent. Or it can declare an emergency and demand 92 percent. It can also raise the effective rate in less noticeable ways, by adjusting deductions and exemptions. (Over the years, inflation has grossly eroded the personal exemption.) There is no certain bulwark against such confiscation. In principle, if not in practice, the income tax authorizes total government. The citizen is nothing more than a revenue producer. If he is permitted to keep anything, it is just so he can continue producing for the government. "Whichever way you turn this [the Sixteenth] amendment," Chodorov wrote, "you come up with the fact that it gives the government a prior lien on all the property produced by its subjects."[14] This is what he meant when he said that the Sixteenth Amendment and the income tax fundamentally changed the relationship between citizen and state in America.

Individual Rights

Chodorov's words aptly lead us into a discussion of individual rights. The argument to this point has assumed that people have rights; in other words, people are individually sovereign in such a way as to make some conduct toward them, even by the state, off-limits. The United States was founded on that notion. Key documents — the Declaration of Independence and the Constitution — refer to rights. Implicit in the idea of rights is that if someone acquires possessions or earns an income, he has a moral claim in that property. That may seem obvious. But it is not self-evident. This is not the place to launch into a full theory of rights, but the outline of such a theory can be offered.[15]

First off, rights are necessary to avert violent conflict, the potential for which, in a world of scarcity, is ever present. Violence is inimical to the human enterprise. To live, human beings must produce, which means, among other things, acquire property. The right to pursue one's life without the right to try to acquire and control property is an absurdity. As long as people are corporeal, property will be at the center of individual rights. All rights can be reduced to property rights, beginning with the property right in one's own body and person.

People cannot think, plan long-term, use resources (property), and produce the things life depends on if they are constantly in fear of predators. Life therefore depends on peaceful coexistence among people. The idea of rights makes the fullest coexistence possible by drawing practical boundaries around each person and his interests. By putting everyone on notice about what constitutes a trespass against others, conflict is averted, or at least strongly discouraged. That in turn lets each person go about the business of living productively. (Of course, to live productively in a modern economy means benefiting others through voluntary exchange and the division of labor.)

Rights therefore are conflict-avoidance principles. Since they are based on the nature of human beings and the nature of the world of scarcity, it is entirely proper to use the term "natural rights." That term also serves to emphasize that rights are not arbitrary conventions or privileges granted by government.

Once we validate the idea of rights, it takes little effort to see that they include the right to whatever one acquires through non-violent, nonfraudulent methods, such as voluntary exchange. In a modern economy, income is acquired through exchange. (The standard distinction between earned income, such as wages, and "unearned" income, such as interest and dividends, is rejected here. All income peacefully acquired is *earned* income because it is the result of exchange with willing traders.) People, whether we call them workers or business owners, exchange goods or services or both for money. Investors give up the use of their money now in anticipation of more later. The upshot is that they all begin with something that is theirs by right — their property or their labor — and exchange it with a willing partner for something else. What is

16

received in exchange by the parties is thus theirs by right.

If people thus have a right to the income that they obtain on the market, then the income tax must violate that right. By passing an income tax, politicians claim the right to seize a portion of what people earn. But since the earners themselves have a natural right to that property, the government's claim is illegitimate. The income tax is an intrusion by government into voluntary exchange between peaceful parties. (That characteristic is shared by other forms of taxation.)

The income tax is but one step removed from government's claiming a right to the people's labor itself. It's uncomfortably close to slavery. If you own the fruit, you almost own the tree. The average American head of family, writes James Bovard, works twenty years for the government to pay his taxes.[16] In practical terms, it may be preferable for the government to seize income rather than to commandeer labor directly. But morally, the difference is not great.

Financial Privacy

The income tax is not simply a matter of the government's seizing income, however. Financial privacy must be compromised as well. If the government claims part of people's earnings, it will obviously claim the right to know how much money each citizen makes. The tax enforcers cannot carry out their mandate from Congress if deprived of that information. So the income tax provides a reason for the government to acquire a huge amount of data about what were once private matters: the sources and amount of people's earnings. Information that one might not want to share with friends or even family members must be shared with the government. And people must not only surrender information about themselves; they must also inform on others. When banks pay interest on savings accounts, they must report to the IRS. Casinos likewise have to report winners.

The moral issue here is the impropriety of government's threatening its citizens with penalties for not surrendering certain personal information. That is a long way from the earlier American notion that government should leave people alone unless they violate the rights of someone else.

An income tax is likely to include withholding; employers are compelled to send part of their workers' pay to the government before the workers even see it. There is something particularly unseemly about tax authorities' getting their hands on people's money that way. Note that tax withholding makes unpaid conscript tax collectors out of employers.

Withholding has an insidious effect on taxpayers. Since they do not get possession of the money before it is taken, the sense of deprivation is vastly diminished or eliminated entirely. And because so many taxpayers have money overwithheld and therefore receive refunds, they often look on the IRS as a benefactor. (To permit over-withholding, of course, is to lend the government money at zero interest.) A former IRS lawyer, Andrew Levine, says he has no doubt "there would be a national revolt against current federal taxes if the public paid them on April 15. Withholding provides the key illusion which allows the tax system to function."[17] Another writer has observed that "withholding is important in cutting the pain of paying."[18]

In other words, withholding enables the government to raise more revenue from the income tax than it otherwise could. Recall Colbert's concern, quoted in chapter 1, about minimizing the hissing of the plucked goose. What does this mean for the morality of the income tax? It indicates that the government has felt compelled to hide the true nature of the tax for fear that citizens would not tolerate it. Withholding also pushes citizens further into the status of slaves, since it embodies the principle that the government has first crack at the fruits of their labor. They are then left with whatever the government thinks they should have. (Withholding will be discussed further in chapter 5.)

Another aspect of the immorality of income taxation is the intimidation the government wields against its citizens. This will be discussed in more detail in chapter 3. Suffice it here to say that income taxation, which requires the government to demand of the taxpayers volumes of personal information, will be based on fear as much as force. In this connection, we should note that the IRS pays people to inform on their fellow citizens about possible tax violations. Author and former IRS official Paul Strassels points out that to fear the taxman is not paranoia. "Nothing is more central to the IRS strategy of tax collection than scaring you, the taxpayer, and keeping you that way," Strassels writes.[19] There is something especially odious about a tax that depends on the government's frightening its citizens.

Why Tax Income?

Fear, withholding, and loss of financial privacy are bound to be part of any income tax. But they are only the beginning of its moral problems. Why tax income? If taxes are seen as the price of vital services, the tax is hard to explain because income is an odd basis for payment. That is particularly true with a graduated, or progressive, income tax. But it is also true of a flat, or proportional, tax.[20] That may come as a surprise, since many people who dislike the graduated income tax prefer the flat tax. With a graduated tax, of course, the tax rate rises as income rises. In contrast, under a flat tax the rate is constant. Someone making $100,000 pays more tax than someone making $30,000, but the proportion of income is the same (ignoring exemptions). It is said to be fairer and more consistent with the rule of law than a progressive tax. Adam Smith was one of its proponents.

But is it fair? We don't pay for other services and products proportionally. A wealthy person pays the same price for Cheerios as a poor person. But that means he pays a smaller percentage of income than the poor person. In the language of taxation, that would be regarded as "regressive," but few people object to that. Only when it comes to government services and taxation do people think the amount paid, if not the proportion, should rise with income.[21]

The flat-rate income tax is perhaps theoretically less bad than the progressive income tax, but it is still bad. First, it is, after all, a tax. Second, as a tax on incomes, the more someone earns, the more it takes. Third, to enforce it, the government will need the appropriate powers.

But we can acknowledge that the progressive tax compounds the evil of the proportional tax by taking an ever larger share as a person's income rises. Thus, we come to what is known as the "ability to pay" principle, though that principle underlies any income tax. Early in the century, the leading promoter of progressive income taxation was the Columbia University professor of political economy Edwin R. A. Seligman. In several books, Seligman strove to link the ability-to-pay principle to the advance of civilization, arguing that other methods were old-fashioned, unfair, and even reactionary. He claimed to be able to "discern the slow laborious growth of standards of justice in taxation, and the attempt on the part of the community to realize this justice." What he saw was "the evolution of the principle of faculty or ability in taxation — the principle that each individual should be held to help the state in proportion to his ability to help himself."[22]

An earlier political philosopher put the same principle this way: from each according to ability, to each according to his need. It of course was Karl Marx. The progressive income tax was part of the program outlined in the *Communist Manifesto*. Seligman undoubtedly would have objected to being called a Marxist. You don't have to be a Marxist to embrace the progressive income tax. Abraham Lincoln, an earlier income taxer, was not a Marxist. Nevertheless, he shared a core principle with Marx: that one's ability to create wealth should be the criterion for how much a person should be forced to surrender to the state. Marx at least was perceptive, or honest, enough to acknowledge that the faculty principle leads to total government.

What of this ability-to-pay principle? We must not lose sight of Rothbard's point that if taxation is unjust per se, the ability-to-pay principle cannot be a principle of justice. Besides, it doesn't prove what its exponents want to prove. You don't need progressive rates for the rich to pay more than the nonrich. Under a flat rate, the rich would also pay more. Even under regressive rates the rich could pay more: 10 percent of $100,000 is more than 25 percent of $10,000.[23]

Finally, the principle is not as clear as it may seem. For example, the income tax hits only income; but someone could have a small income and great accumulated wealth. Who has more "ability to pay"? (Switching to a wealth tax would sabotage the economic system in the name of justice.) Seligman defended the principle on the grounds that the more money someone has, the easier it is to make money. Here he was suggesting that wealthy people don't have to exert effort to satisfy consumers. We know that is not true. Fortunes can be lost.[24]

Rothbard notes that the ability-to-pay principle implies that we can compare the value of a dollar for different people and conclude that someone with more dollars values each one less than someone with fewer. That may have some intuitive appeal. But there is no scientific way to establish that claim. The ranking of values is subjective for each person.[25]

Related to ability-to-pay is the benefits principle: people who make more money get more protection from government and therefore should pay proportionately more in taxes. But even if we could measure subjective benefits, one can as easily argue the opposite of what is usually assumed. People with many resources would be better able to take care of themselves in the absence of government protection than those with meager resources. Rothbard points out that a rich man's assets could be more compact and less costly to protect than a poor farmer's land. Poor people therefore arguably gain proportionately greater benefits from government than wealthy people. Does the benefits principle mean that poor people pay more than the rich?[26]

The only system that really links (subjective) benefits to payment is the free market, where freedom of choice is the rule. People are free to abstain from buying something if its expected benefits rank beneath those provided by some other use of the money. Government is based on the opposite principle — coercion.

Are We the State?

In the end, the benefits principle undercuts the ability principle. And Seligman knew it. If he was to win people over to the ability principle, he would have to argue against the benefits principle. He wrote that a person "does not measure the benefits of state action to himself ... because ... such measurement implies a decidedly erroneous conception of the relationship of the individual to the modern state." Demonstrating a presumptuousness not uncommon among certain economists, Seligman proclaimed that "it is now generally agreed that we pay taxes not because the state protects us, or because we get any benefits from the state, but simply because the state is part of us."[27]

That is a remarkable statement. The state, in Seligman's view, is not a dispenser of useful public services, payment for which is to be based on benefits received. The state is something else, an almost-mystical part of ourselves. That idea can be traced to the philosophy of Jean Jacques Rousseau and others, whose theory of the general will as embodied in the state has done so much to shape modern thinking about democracy. According to that view, collective decision-making through the polity represents the true will and common good of the people as a whole. The implication is that when people act individually in the market they are "selfish" and possibly detrimental to the common good. But when they act as members of the political community, they are mysteriously led to behave as faithful wards of the public interest. You can see the same sentiment expressed in newspaper editorials and syndicated columns after every election day.

That view of the political world has been shown as naive by the public-choice school of political economy, which argues that voters, officeholders, and bureaucrats are the same kind of people as those who exist in the marketplace: they tend to seek personal benefits at the lowest cost. What distinguishes the marketplace from the political arena is not the motives of the actors, but rather the incentives they face. In the market, people understand that they face the costs of their actions. In the political arena, the objective is

21

to get someone else to pay for your benefits. Two great political philosophers have summed up that point: Frederic Bastiat, the nineteenth-century political economist, wrote that the state is the great
fiction by which everyone tries to live at everyone else's expense.[28]
H. L. Mencken, an equally astute observer, wrote in the twentieth
century that "government is a broker in pillage, and every election
is a sort of advance auction sale of stolen goods."[29] Both understood
that the state, rather than being a service provider for society, is primarily a machine for the transfer of wealth from the many to the
favored interests and that the tax system is the principal method of
carrying out that function.

Notice that Seligman claims that most people agree with his
corporativist view of the state. (The corporativist view holds that
society, with the state at the head, is analogous to a single organism,
with one set of interests that constitute the common good. That view
underlies all statism, including the most virulent forms, fascism and
communism.) Was he correct? In the first decades of the twentieth
century most people probably did not believe that the government,
particularly the federal government, was part of them and vice versa;
they were still essentially individualists in the spirit of the American Revolution. Corporativism is a profoundly un-American idea,
since it denies individual sovereignty. When Seligman was tout-
ing corporativism, Mencken was exciting throngs of readers with
a far different position on the nature of government. For Seligman,
government was part of us. For Mencken, government "is really
something imposed from without.... Its interests and those of the
people it governs are the same only occasionally, and then usually
accidentally."[30]

Of course, Seligman was writing in the Progressive Era, when
the intellectual class turned to the corporativist view of the state.
The Progressive Era was a watershed in American history, when
intellectuals, politicians, and bureaucrats, enamored of Bismarck's
welfare state in Germany, fundamentally changed American society by systematically expanding the coercive power of government
while shrinking the power of people over their own lives.[31]

The progressive income tax was part of a campaign to redefine
the moral and political relationship between the American citizen
and the federal government. Before the Progressive era, the U.S.
government played a small role in the lives of Americans. But beginning in the late nineteenth century, with the rise of Progressiv-
ism, that role grew dramatically. Economic relations were managed
from Washington as never before. The Interstate Commerce Com-

mission, Food and Drug Administration, Federal Trade Commission, Federal Reserve System, and other agencies were set up. The permanent income tax was the crowning achievement of the Progressive movement.

A few voices, such as that of the economist David A. Wells, morally objected to the progressive tax. They said it was socialistic. Seligman replied that the "cry of 'socialism' has always been the last refuge of those who wish to clog the wheel of social progress or to prevent the abolition of long-continued abuses."[32]

Seligman also responded to constitutional objections to the income tax by invoking what is now known as the "living Constitution" argument. He said our view of the Constitution must change with the needs of political and social life. "Sooner or later," he said, "we shall outgrow many of the notions of extreme individualism and of exaggerated [States'] rights which dominated the country at the time of the formation of the constitution. They are bound to disappear as they have disappeared in every other great federal republic."[33]

Thus, for Seligman, a father of the U.S. income tax, the principles that inspired the founding of the great American republic were antiquated and in need of replacement. The power to tax incomes could not be denied to the U.S. government because of those extreme notions. He went so far as to suggest that opponents of the income-tax amendment were close to advocating national suicide. "But surely no patriot," he said "can afford to object to conferring upon the United States a power ... without which its prosperity — nay, even its very existence — might possibly be menaced."[34]

Seligman did not feel obliged to explain why the ability principle was the right basis for taxation. For him it was enough to merely assert that it was modern and progressive, as though that were self-evident. That strategy is used by welfare-state activists to this day. Call something progressive, and many people will be afraid to oppose it for fear of being called reactionary. Advocates of the income tax are confident they can portray their opponents as apologists for the rich. Their own interests are never called into question.

Thus it is worth noting that those who argued most strongly for the tax and the corporativist view of government had the most power, wealth, and prestige to gain. The intellectuals who spoke of the need to expand state power could count on manning or advising the bureaus that would exercise that power. Some prominent businessmen, apprehensive about the rigors and uncertainty of free-market competition, joined them in the crusade for bigger government.[35]

Seligman's defense of the income tax — that the state is us — is better looked on as public-relations rhetoric. It is hard to believe that the Progressives really took it seriously. Surely they understood that their programs were devised by a small subset of society — not the whole people — and had the effect of taking decision-making power from the hands of individuals. They might have sincerely thought that government agencies would act in the interest of the people; but surely they realized that the people themselves would not exercise the power. How was that consistent with the claim that the people are the state?

Envy As the Basis of the Income Tax

In reality, what the ability principle means is simply that people who have more should pay more — because they have more. Such is the belief of organizations like Citizens for Tax Justice, which, as economist Roy E. Cordato has noted, never get around to defining "tax justice."[36] From their opposition to a flat-rate tax, we can infer what it means: it isn't enough for the rich to pay more; they must pay *a lot* more. Why? Devotees of the ability principle might like the classic obscurantist response: for those who understand, no explanation is necessary; for those who don't, no explanation is possible.

The upshot is that some people take it for granted that those who have more should be forced to share with those who have less. The Progressive Policy Institute, a so-called moderate think tank tied to the Democratic Party, says, "The point of progressive taxation is not to penalize those who succeed, but to protect those who have not." PPI doesn't want the tax system to treat people equally, because they "may be dealt very different resources with which to compete."[37] Note the misunderstanding. In the free market people aren't "dealt" resources like cards. Many individual voluntary transactions bring about the arrangement of resources in a free society. If by "resources," PPI means intelligence, talent, and ambition, it is not the fault of those who have more that others have less. Despite what PPI says, the only way to "protect" those with less is to take from — that is, penalize — those with more.

PPI goes on to argue, with an interesting twist, that progressive taxation is the appropriate price to pay to have a free market. Since hard work is not the only reason people succeed — talent and things like culture play a role — PPI says, "Our commitment to free markets, while disposing the United States to harsher economic inequalities, also can oblige those who benefit so much from them to contribute more as well."[38] To paraphrase, since wealth might require more than effort, successful people must buy their freedom by paying off the less successful. That is a non sequitur. Even if hard work were the only cause of success, there would be income inequalities. How exactly do the other causes "oblige" the successful to pay more? And how do the successful benefit more from free markets than the less successful? On the contrary, the *less* successful benefit proportionally more from economic freedom than do the well-off. It was the free market that ushered in production for large numbers of people and raised their living standards to unprecedented heights. Besides, as already pointed out, the rich would pay more even under some regressive tax rates. So PPI has not made a case that fairness requires progressivity. Yet such nonsense is typical for the phony fairness crowd.

It is one thing to hold charity as a virtue; it is quite another to turn it into a political principle. How easily people slide from thinking that charity is good to thinking that charity ought to be compelled by government. They apparently never grasped George Washington's reputed statement, "Government is not reason, it is not eloquence; it is force. Like fire, it is a dangerous servant and a fearful master." Because of its coercive nature, government transmogrifies commonplace activities into something hideous. At the hands of the government, trade becomes extortion, religion becomes the Inquisition, and education becomes brainwashing. Forced charity is theft, regardless of motive.

Worse than using the tax system to force some to pay for government services for others is the attempt to use it to level incomes and combat inequality. A well-known economist of decades ago, Henry C. Simons, wrote that income taxation is an "instrument of economic control, a means of mitigating economic inequality." He called for "drastic progression in taxation" because he was offended ethically and even aesthetically by "the prevailing distribution of wealth and income."[39] Many people believe this today. But to repeat: in a market economy, income is not "distributed" in any real sense. No central distributor ladles it from a common pot. Rather, it is obtained through countless voluntary transactions, each of which must be regarded as grounded in justice. Once that fact is grasped, the rhetoric of fairness in taxation is revealed as demagoguery. One is hard-pressed to see how an income "distribution" that resulted from voluntary exchange can be, in Simons's word, "unlovely."[40] He had a right to his ethical and aesthetic judgments, of course; but

25

he was not justified in calling on the force of law to impose his judgments.

Where there is freedom there is disparity of incomes. That is true because of the ever-present principle of natural diversity. People are different in all kinds of ways, inborn and environmental — and those differences will generate differences in incomes. Government attempts to iron out those differences will not only interfere with personal freedom; they will also discourage people from using their talents and resources to satisfy consumers. As Adam Smith wrote in *The Wealth of Nations*, it is not from the benevolence of others that we expect goods and services but from their regard for their own interests. In that case, then, all people, particularly those with lower incomes, will be worse off when people good at producing wealth are taxed. (Chapter 4 will explain this point in more detail.)

To put this another way, higher incomes do not come at the expense of those with lower incomes. No injustice, or unfairness, is indicated by income disparities generated in the marketplace. On the contrary, justice (if that is what fairness means) entails letting people keep and control their property. All the obfuscation concerning tax fairness is intended to hide that piece of common sense.

Another wrinkle in the fairness issue is the concern over whether income groups pay their "fair share." Again, the fair-share advocates refuse to reveal their standard of judgment. All we know is that they think the top groups should pay more.[41]

But how much is enough? IRS data show that the top filers already pay most of the tax. In 1994 the top 1 percent of filers paid as much as the bottom 80 percent.[42]

You would think that the fair-share advocates would be delighted that upper-income people pay so much. But they aren't delighted. No amount is enough for them. Besides, what seems to disturb them is that the high portion of tax paid resulted from *cuts* in marginal tax rates. It seems the more that marginal rates are cut for the top filers, the larger their share of tax paid. The converse is also true: raise rates and the top filers as a group pay less.

The top marginal rate dropped twice between 1979 and 1988: from 70 percent to 50 percent in the early 1980s and to 28 percent in the late 1980s. The fair-share advocates opposed those cuts. Yet that is when the percentage of total revenues paid by the rich began to rise after decades of decline. Presidents Bush and Clinton both raised the top rate, to 31 percent and nearly 40 percent, respectively. Predictably, the share of taxes paid by the top earners fell slightly.[43]

The fair-share advocates scoff at those numbers by pointing

out that the top filers also made more money. Oh horror! But isn't that the point? Income taxes discourage the creation of wealth. It is hard to avoid the conclusion that so-called tax fairness is really motivated by envy toward those who earn more. The rhetoric of fairness shrouds something far less attractive: a resentment against people with the talent, foresight, and ambition to succeed beyond the average and to be rewarded for it. When you come right down to it, envy is a major reason for the income tax.

A final dimension of the morality issue: more than one observer has noted that the income tax may well erode personal morality. People have a natural interest in keeping as much of their income as they can. Deep down, many do not believe it is wrong to hide information or income from the IRS. The problem is that that attitude may not be directed only to the tax authorities. People who think less than carefully may feel that if it isn't really wrong to "cheat" the taxman, maybe it isn't wrong to cheat others either. If so, part of our cultural decline can be attributable to the income tax.[44]

In moral terms, the income tax is a disaster. It deprives people of their property, punishes success, violates their financial privacy, makes them pawns in social engineering and income-leveling schemes, and interferes with their ethical compass. It is unfit for a free society.

In the next chapter, we will see how it turns citizens into subjects.

Notes

¹ Quoted in David Burnham, *A Law Unto Itself: Power, Politics and the IRS* (New York: Random House, 1989), p. 7.

² Frank Chodorov, *The Income Tax: Root of All Evil* (New York: Devin-Adair, 1954).

³ Ibid., pp. 5, 6.

⁴ Ibid., pp. 6, 8.

⁵ Quoted in James L. Payne, *Costly Returns: The Burdens of the U.S. Tax System* (San Francisco: ICS Press, 1993), p. 129.

⁶ Quoted in James Bovard, *Lost Rights: The Destruction of American Liberty* (New York: St. Martin's Griffin, 1995), p. 265.

⁷ Quoted in Payne, p. 103.

⁸ Murray N. Rothbard, *Power and Market: Government and the Economy* (Kansas City, Mo.: Sheed Andrews and McMeel, 1977), p. 136. Rothbard returned to his critique of Smith in *Economic Thought Before Adam Smith: An Austrian Perspective on the History of Economic Thought*, vol. 1 (Brookfield, Vt.: Edward Elgar Publishing Co., 1995), pp. 469–71.

⁹ Rothbard, *Power and Market*, pp. 141–44.

¹⁰ See, for example, William F. Shughart II, ed., *Taxing Choice: The Predatory Politics of Fiscal Discrimination* (New Brunswick, N.J.: Transaction Publishers, 1996).

¹¹ Jean-Baptiste Say, *A Treatise on Political Economy* (1803; New York: Augustus M. Kelley, 1971), p. 416, footnote. Here Say sounds a little like the late-nineteenth-century American constitutional lawyer Lysander Spooner, who likened the state to a highwayman.

¹² Ibid. For a rare analysis of Say's view on taxation, see Murray N. Rothbard, *Classical Economics: An Austrian Perspective on the History of Economic Thought*, vol. 2 (Brookfield, Vt.: Edward Elgar Publishing Co., 1995), pp. 40–43.

¹³ Frank Chodorov, *One Is a Crowd* (New York: Devin-Adair, 1952), p. 154.

¹⁴ Chodorov, *Income Tax,* p. 12.

¹⁵ Much good work has been done in validating individual rights. Among others, see Ayn Rand, "Man's Rights" in *Capitalism: The Unknown Ideal* (New York: New American Library, 1967), pp. 286–94; Tibor Machan, *Individuals and Their Rights* (LaSalle, Ill.: Open Court, 1989); and Douglas B. Rasmussen and Douglas J. Den Uyl, *Liberty and Nature: An Aristotelian Defense of Liberal*

Order (LaSalle, Ill.: Open Court, 1991). For an excellent introduction to libertarianism, the philosophy of individual liberty, see David Boaz, *Libertarianism: A Primer* (New York: Free Press, 1997).

[16] Bovard, p. 289.

[17] Quoted in Burnham, p. 28.

[18] John S. Carroll, "How Taxpayers Think About Their Taxes: Frames and Values" in Joel Slemrod, ed., *Why People Pay Taxes: Tax Compliance and Enforcement* (Ann Arbor, Mich.: The University of Michigan Press, 1992), p. 49.

[19] Quoted in Payne, p. 130.

[20] In truth, since all "flat tax" proposals include a personal exemption, they are not really flat taxes. They include two tax rates, zero and whatever rate has been set for incomes above the exemption.

[21] Rothbard, *Power and Market*, pp. 145, 148.

[22] Edwin R. A. Seligman, *Essays in Taxation,* 9th ed. (New York: Macmillan, 1923), p. 18. The earlier editions predated the constitutional amendment permitting a federal income tax.

[23] My thanks to Professor Roy E. Cordato of Campbell University for this point.

[24] Rothbard, *Power and Market*, pp. 144–46.

[25] Ibid., pp. 149–50.

[26] See ibid., pp. 154–55.

[27] Seligman, pp. 72–73.

[28] See Frederic Bastiat, *The Law* (1850; Irvington, N.Y.: Foundation for Economic Education, 1996).

[29] H. L. Mencken, *A Carnival of Buncombe,* ed. Malcolm Moos (Baltimore: The Johns Hopkins Press, 1956), p. 325.

[30] H. L. Mencken *Prejudices: Sixth Series* (New York: Knopf, 1927), pp. 53–54; quoted in Mayo DuBasky, *The Gist of Mencken: Quotations from America's Critic* (Metuchen, N.J.: The Scarecrow Press, 1990), pp. 383–84.

[31] The leading German state, Prussia, adopted the progressive income tax in 1851, before Bismarck unified and became chancellor of Germany. Prussia was not the first modern state to adopt the income tax. That distinction goes to Great Britain, which started taxing incomes in order to defeat Napoleon. Charles Adams, *For Good and Evil: The Impact of Taxes on the Course of Civilization* (Lanham, Md.: Madison Books, 1993), pp. 343 ff.

[32] Edwin R. A. Seligman, *The Income Tax: A Study of the History, Theory, and Practice of Income Taxation at Home and Abroad*, 2nd ed. rev. (New York: Macmillan, 1921), p. 518. He pointed out that the same objection had been made to factory regulation and government schooling.

[33] Ibid., pp. 618–19.

[34] Ibid., p. 628.

[35] See Gabriel Kolko, *The Triumph of Conservatism: A Reinterpretation of American History, 1900–1916* (Chicago: Quadrangle Books, 1967).

[36] Roy E. Cordato, "Tax Fairness or Moral Bankruptcy," IRET Policy Bulletin, no. 53, September 6, 1991, Institute for Research on the Economics of Taxation, Washington, D.C.

[37] "The Case for Tax Fairness: Talking Points," April 1996, at the Democratic Leadership Council–Progressive Policy Institute website: www.dlcppi.org/texts/economic/ftaxtkp.htm.

[38] Ibid.

[39] Henry C. Simons, *Personal Income Taxation* (Chicago: University of Chicago Press, 1938), pp. 18–19; quoted in Cordato, p. 6. Strangely, Simons called himself a libertarian.

[40] See Robert Nozick, *Anarchy, State, and Utopia* (New York: Basic Books, 1974).

[41] Cordato, pp. 10–11.

[42] The table below summarizes the point that upper-income groups pay the bulk of the personal income tax. What's more, over the last fifteen years, as marginal rates have fallen, the top filers have seen their share of the tax increase.

Proportion of the Federal Income Tax by Income Group, 1995

	Share of AGI	Share of Taxes
Top 1%	14.6%	30.2%
Top 5%	28.8	48.9
Top 10%	40.2	60.5
Top 25%	63.4	80.3
Top 50%	85.5	95.4
Bottom 50%	14.5	4.6

Source: The Tax Foundation, www.taxfoundation.org/prtopincomechart2.html.

[43] "Top Income Earners Continue to Shoulder Greater Share of Income," no date, at The Tax Foundation website: www.taxfoundation.org/prtopincome.html.

[44] Payne, pp. 145–47.

3

Who's the Master?
Who's the Servant?

There was a time in the United States when people generally felt they were the master and the government was the servant. Indeed, that libertarian spirit was the legacy of the revolutionary generation, which had been appalled by its experience with the British crown's treatment of the colonies. Under the colonial regime, arbitrary rule — including a series of intrusive taxes — exacted a painful toll, leading to an unprecedented revolutionary movement. That movement declared that human beings have rights antecedent to government, that government's purpose is the protection of those rights, and that if government itself became inimical to liberty, the people were justified in altering or abolishing it. It would be impossible to overstate how novel and radical that moment in history was. The United States of America was the first nation self-consciously created for the sake of the individual.

The achievement of the War for Independence was to be an end to arbitrary rule, a respect for the rights of man, and a government that was kept in its place not only by a formal constitution but also by the unwritten constitution in the hearts and minds of the people. Despite some serious contradictions of the libertarian philosophy, the most egregious being slavery, the United States became the freest — and, not coincidentally, the most prosperous — society on earth. Even after an unfortunate accumulation of power in the Civil War, the United States of the 1870s still showed great promise for the future as a beacon of liberty.

But something went wrong. Today, the people are not the master. The government is not the servant. Somewhere along the way, the Founders' accomplishment was turned on its head. Many factors contributed to that change. But one thing stands out. In 1913, the Sixteenth Amendment to the U.S. Constitution was adopted. That amendment permitted the federal government to levy taxes on incomes. Although the first tax passed under that amendment affected only a small number of citizens, a virulent germ had been planted in the body politic. That germ would grow and become more powerful, to the point where it would fundamentally redefine the relationship between the American citizen and the federal government. Do you need a dramatic demonstration of that point? The IRS pays people to inform on their neighbors about possible tax violations. What would the Founders have said about that?

More than anything else perhaps, the Sixteenth Amendment and the income tax killed the Old Republic.

This chapter will look at how the income tax has shaped the relationship between the American people and the U.S. government, particularly the IRS, which is charged with collection of the income tax. (We will focus on the personal income tax, though the issues apply as well to the corporate income tax and that other income tax, the payroll tax that finances Social Security.) Readers should bear in mind right from the start that the evils to be described are not incidental to the taxation of income. They are intrinsic. The moment the government is permitted to tax incomes, a dynamic is unleashed that must undermine individual liberty despite the stated intentions of the policymakers. The only way to end that daily assault on liberty is to abolish the taxation of income in all its forms. It should become clear in due course why the American people would experience a quantum leap in freedom and prosperity if the IRS and income tax were abolished.

No Consent of the Governed

We should note up front that the system about to be described cannot be said to have had the public's consent — despite the nominally democratic form of government we live under. Author James Payne writes that it "has been implemented quietly and incrementally by a handful of tax administrators and senior members of congressional committees" — without public debate, much less knowledge.[1] There is no sense in which the people chose the system they are saddled with. How was it adopted? It was adopted piecemeal over many years, primarily after consultation between inter-

34

ested parties in and outside the government and members of the tax-writing committees. The public interest is not what motivated those people. They were more concerned with making it easiser for the IRS to bring in the money. (Any outsiders were seeking special treatment only for themselves.) The bulk of taxpayers, on the other hand, were unorganized and too busy raising their families and making a living to become informed on the complex issues and to voice their objections.

Most tax measures are highly technical. Many are tacked on to other legislation. The majority of members of Congress are barely aware of them. How many even read the bills? Only occasionally does a tax issue get the public's attention and prompt its wrath. In the early 1980s, Congress passed a measure requiring the withholding of tax on bank interest. After it was in the law, banks and savers became enraged and lobbied until the measure was repealed.[2] But that was highly unusual. The vast majority of tax changes slip quietly into law. Almost all are skewed against the taxpayers at large. It is a sad story for a country of such noble origins. Surely that is not what the Founders meant by self-government.

The problem of public consent aside, a central point about the system is this: when government is permitted to tax income, it inevitably acquires a variety of powers to obtain personal information about the people's lives and income-producing activities and to intimidate citizens into complying with its rules. An effective income tax without such powers would be impossible. The government insists the tax system is voluntary. Does anyone really believe that? An IRS official, Charles Gibb, once said that those who believe the tax system is voluntary probably also believe in the tooth fairy.[3] True, the IRS relies on the taxpayers (and their employers and banks and others) to provide the bulk of the information it needs to carry out its mission. But it has an arsenal of weapons to ensure that the taxpayers do so and to punish them afterwards if they don't. Just remember: if you don't pay, the IRS can seize your money and your home; it can wreck your credit record; it can imprison you! George Orwell would understand how the taxmen use the word *voluntary*.

A second key point about the tax system is that the federal government, with its $1.6 trillion budget, has an insatiable appetite for revenue. It is a wealth-transfer machine. The dispensing of money from taxpayers to favored interests is the central activity of officeholders and bureaucrats. Their careers depend on it. Thus, they need an uninterrupted flow of money to the U.S. Treasury. Nothing must be permitted to interfere with it. Once that is understood, much else becomes clear. Because of that need for money, the U.S. Congress has endowed the IRS with vast powers and freedom of action. We should be surprised if the IRS did not zealously pursue its objectives and treat the taxpayers as farm animals in the process. The courts have also shown great deference to the IRS. As David Burnham observed in 1989, "The Congress, the courts, and the agency itself have over the years passed hundreds of laws, handed down thousands of decisions, and issued uncounted numbers of regulations that together have molded the IRS into a genuinely formidable organization. In fact, with the probable exception of a handful of agencies in the Soviet Union and China, there is little question that the IRS today is the single most powerful bureaucracy in the world."[4]

The IRS enforces nearly 20,000 ever-changing pages of arcane law and regulations. The Internal Revenue Manual is 260 volumes of fine print. The tax code is like a monster amoeba constantly changing shape just when you think you may understand it. Daniel Pilla, an expert on the tax system, points out that the 1980s saw the tax laws changed more than one hundred times. The allegedly historic tax simplification of 1986 "brought amendments to more than 2,000 sections of the code and the creation of more than 100 new forms. To teach us about those forms, the IRS produces thousands of pages of instructions, and hundreds of booklets to teach us about the instructions."[5]

Advantage Government

A tax code that is constantly in flux at once puts the citizen at a gross disadvantage with the government. No one can master that body of arcane provisions. Professional tax preparers routinely differ over what they mean. IRS employees themselves cannot agree and typically give out conflicting information to taxpayers. This problem was recognized as early as 1913, the year the tax was enacted, when the influential U.S. senator Elihu Root of New York half-joked that he and all his friends might end up in jail for not understanding the new income tax law.[6] It has only gotten worse. An IRS instructor once said that errors could be found in 99 percent of all tax returns. And journalist David Burnham notes, "The reality that so many are somehow in violation of a supremely murky law gives the agency and the individual agent an astonishingly free hand to pick and choose their targets."[7]

Disagreements among IRS personnel and tax preparers make

funny newspaper stories. But think about what it really means. The existence of a fluid tome full of technical commandments is an attack on the rule of law, which is supposed to protect citizens from arbitrary governance. Among other guarantees, the rule of law, a pillar of Western civilization, promises that the legal rules that are binding on all citizens will be clear and knowable in advance. The law is not supposed to be a snare waiting to nab unsuspecting people as they go about their peaceful business. Yet the tax code is just that. The existence of such a code cannot help but instill in the people a sense of inferiority and timidity with respect to the government, attitudes contrary to the popular and individual sovereignty that is supposed to characterize the American system. Each person may suspect that he has probably already broken the law unintentionally. No one could pass the scrutiny of the tax agents except by the dumbest luck. The feared audit is our modern-day version of the Inquisition. The threat that the authorities could someday examine anyone's tax records can have a chilling effect on a citizen's willingness to assert his rights. The income tax over time has helped to turn the American people from a rambunctious group of revolutionaries, protective of their liberty, into a herd of sheep fearful of offending those in power.

By the same token, this situation must engender in the IRS a sense of awesome superiority over the citizens. An IRS agent told David Burnham that she and her colleagues often referred to the public as "slime" or "deadbeats."[8] In the eyes of the tax agents, everyone is a potential suspect and conquest in a grand cat-and-mouse game. An anonymous tax agent (using the pen name Diogenes) wrote a book in 1973 called *The April Game*, in which he related how he and his fellow agents intimidated taxpayers by the sheer power they possessed. The author referred to his employer as "an American Gestapo." "There is hardly an American citizen above the poverty level whose tax conscience is so completely clear that he isn't scared of being audited," he wrote. "Of all the information-gathering agencies in all the world's governments, past or present, the very cleverest must surely be the United States Internal Revenue Service. That monster organization gathers more information about more people, does it more quietly and raises less public outcry in the process than any other government outfit I know anything about."[9]

No one should be surprised by any of that. What is more in accord with human nature than for a person to try to keep what is rightfully his? The mission of the IRS is to thwart that manifestation of human nature. That requires extraordinary powers.

In carrying out its mission, the IRS holds nearly all the cards. Frank Chodorov wrote that the IRS "has a war against society on its hands, and to win that war it must make use of the artifices of war, such as espionage, deception, and force."[10] Lord Acton's dictum comes to mind: power tends to corrupt, and absolute power corrupts absolutely.[11] The "S" in IRS may stand for "service," but let's face it: service is not what the agency provides, despite its public rhetoric about the taxpayers' being its customers. The IRS has more power to control the activities of the American people than any other agency of government.[12] Its power also makes it irresistible to political leaders who might like to make life difficult for the people who cross them.

A case in point is the use of the IRS by presidents to harass political opponents. In early 1997 the *Washington Post* reported that President Nixon sought a "ruthless son of a bitch" as head of the IRS so he could go after his enemies.[13] It wasn't the first time a president used the agency for political gain. Unpopular tax-exempt organizations have also felt the brunt of the IRS's powers. (As this is written, conservative organizations are being audited.) Such use of the IRS is obviously improper.[14] It should be emphasized, however, that the IRS is not dangerous primarily because of its power to engage in political investigations. Outrageous as those violations of civil liberties are, scarier are the routine, everyday threats against citizens that are not politically motivated. They are inherent in the tax system, although that fact is unappreciated.[15]

The IRS Arsenal

The IRS's arsenal of weapons against the taxpayers is truly awesome. The IRS has the usual panoply of criminal law-enforcement powers at its disposal. But that is only the beginning of the story. It files a relatively small number of criminal charges each year against taxpayers. More significant are its unique civil powers. David Burnham says, "Over the years, the IRS's quiver has been stuffed with a much larger number of very sharp enforcement arrows than have been granted to any other law enforcement agency in the United States."[16] That in itself indicates how important revenue raising is to the lawmakers, who are responsible for the IRS's power.

Because of the long Anglo-American legal tradition protective of individual rights, when the government suspects someone of a crime, it must comply with many requirements intended to keep citizens from being victimized by capricious conduct. The state must specify charges and follow long-standing procedures designed to safeguard liberty. Most important, it must assume the burden of proof. A criminal suspect is innocent until proven guilty beyond a reasonable doubt. The suspect has no legal burden to demonstrate his innocence. The Fifth Amendment to the U.S. Constitution protects his rights. The placement of the burden on the government derives from the principle that a negative cannot be proved. A world in which the government could charge someone with a crime and then demand that he prove he did not commit it would be a nightmare.

Unfortunately, that nightmare is real with respect to the IRS. Its power to bring civil, along with criminal, charges relieves it of much of the burden that the FBI and the local police force shoulder. The IRS has the power to charge taxpayers with *civil* violations and then, without outside review, impose huge fines, seize property, and place liens on assets. A citizen has the legal right to challenge the IRS — however expensive that process might be. But he may not get an injunction to halt IRS action while he has a hearing. Moreover, the onus is on him to prove that he committed no offense. Thus, the traditional burden of proof is turned on its head. According to surveys, the legal burden, the expense, and the complexity of the law discourage taxpayers from filing appeals.[17] As a matter of principle, this is an outrageous state of affairs in a country that prides itself on being free. It is made worse by the fact that the IRS bases many civil cases on erroneous calculations and other carelessness. The IRS doesn't get audited very often. But when it has been audited, its error rate, not to mention its rate of noncompliance with its own procedures, has been large.[18]

Burnham, author Martin Gross, and journalist James Bovard tell many hair-raising stories of how callous or corrupt tax agents have made life a living hell for taxpayers who had done nothing wrong. The government's own General Accounting Office estimated in 1990 that the IRS made more than 50,000 erroneous levies on citizens and firms annually. It seems the IRS too often neglects to record tax payments. Thus the IRS may seize a bank account because it didn't realize a taxpayer had already paid what was demanded of him.[19]

Burnham writes that "because IRS supervisors have little time to review the actual day-to-day decisions of revenue officers, and because the legal guidelines laid down by Congress are almost never precise, and because judicial approval is not required before the

IRS acts, and because Congress has sharply limited the right of the courts to review IRS enforcement actions after the fact, there is significant room for abuse in how the IRS exercises those powers.[20] Note that Burnham refers to the courts' limited oversight of the IRS. The traditional checks and balances on which the U.S. government was initially founded have been largely suspended in the case of the IRS, which is often "policeman, prosecutor, judge, and executioner."[21] That's not how the American system was supposed to work.

Citizen Recourse Limited

The recourse available to citizens who have been abused by government has long been severely restricted by the old doctrine of sovereign immunity, which limits the right to sue the state. In tax matters the right to sue has been virtually nonexistent; the IRS was specifically excluded from the Federal Tort Claims Act, which permitted some suits against the government. The 1988 Taxpayers' Bill of Rights permits some taxpayer suits against the IRS. But the right to sue is still subject to strict limitation. For example, a wronged taxpayer has to show that the tax agent was reckless or malicious, elements that at best are very difficult to prove. The bill provided some other small safeguards for taxpayers. But James Payne was unimpressed. "My reading of this law," he writes, "indicates that most of its provisions are advisory and that IRS officials can ignore them if they so choose."[22] Broader protections for taxpayers could not pass because members of Congress and others believe such measures would undermine the IRS's ability to keep the money rolling in. That in fact is what IRS commissioners and their predecessors unfailingly say when they testify against giving taxpayers more legal protection.[23]

In 1996, a somewhat broader Taxpayers' Bill of Rights did pass the Congress, which, among other things, expanded the Office of Taxpayer Advocate to give it more authority to resolve taxpayer difficulties. But Gross warns that it "cannot change the basic problem with the IRS system."[24] David Keating, president of the National Taxpayers Union, which lobbied for the bill of rights, conceded that "the job of protecting taxpayer rights is far from finished." Keating added that "vague, complex tax laws allow abuses, and allow the IRS to make a plausible case against anyone."[25]

As a result of Senate Finance Committee hearings in the fall of 1997, Congress was once again looking at IRS procedures and taxpayer rights. The hearings, which presented the testimony of victims of IRS abuse, led the House of Representatives to overwhelmingly pass a bill calling for an overhaul of the agency. Among other things, the bill would shift the burden of proof in court cases (not audits) to the IRS. However, taxpayers would still be required to cooperate with "reasonable" requests of the agency. The bill would create an eleven-member board of private citizens to oversee various aspects of the IRS, such as long-range planning. It would also increase the authority of the Office of the Taxpayer Advocate.[26]

It must be pointed out that such reforms are inherently limited, given the mission of the IRS, which is to collect a huge amount of money from the American people. Moreover, the law of unintended consequences must not be ignored. Shifting the burden of proof to the IRS sounds like a protaxpayer step, but it could backfire. If the IRS is to sustain its burden, it will most likely be permitted wide latitude to subpoena records from taxpayers and third parties. In the end, it still may be difficult to tell who really has the burden of proof. The danger of this "reform" is a further indication that the core of the IRS is intrinsically abusive of citizens and is therefore not something that can be fixed with halfway measures.

Even some people within the IRS think the agency is overbearing and oppressive. IRS managers who were surveyed in the late 1980s "generally viewed" the agency as "too authoritarian" and "dictatorial." Part of that attitude has resulted from agents' having enforcement quotas to fulfill, though that practice has in theory been eliminated.[27] Agents have also been rewarded on the basis of how much property they seize from taxpayers. "The IRS imposes almost no controls over its own agents' property seizures," James Bovard writes.[28]

As a result, in the 1990s the IRS was imposing more than thirty million penalties and more than three million levies on bank accounts and wages annually.[29] Numbers of that magnitude, not to mention the IRS's frightening error rate, are what prompted a few members of Congress to provide the meager protection that has been passed.[30]

James Payne points out that the power to seize bank accounts and property instills in IRS agents an arrogance completely out of keeping with a free society and limited government. He catalogues IRS practices, such as seizing assets leased but not owned by taxpayers, that are intended purely to inflict pain, since they may not even produce revenue for the government.[31]

Unsurprisingly, the IRS dislikes oversight from the Congress. A 1991 survey indicated that three out of four managers at the agency feel justified in lying when they testify in Congress. Bovard cites a *Roll Call* report that said that "only 47 percent of the managers feel the need to be 'completely honest' when testifying before a Congressional committee — and the number drops to 24 percent when appearing before a committee chaired by a 'critical or headline-seeking chairman.'"[32] This is simply another case in which tax agents have "rights" that are denied other citizens. Anyone else who lies while testifying under oath is subject to sanctions. Here's another case of special treatment: taxpayers may not give a false name to tax authorities. Yet tax agents are permitted to lie about their identity to the taxpayers.[33]

Apparently, the IRS doesn't like anyone looking over its shoulder. When its own staff historian tried to examine internal agency records, she was investigated and hounded out of her job. Shelley L. Davis discovered that the IRS had been destroying records in violation of the law. She recalled that during her seven years at the IRS, "I saw how the agency operates in an autocratic, fear-driven environment, with shocking disregard for the well-being of those it so much likes to call its 'customers,' in other words you, the taxpayer." In the name of protecting taxpayers, she said, the IRS denies citizens access to information on how it operates. She calls the IRS "the government's most secretive agency."[34]

Civil Liberties Ignored

It would be helpful now to see up close how awesome the IRS's power is over the average citizen. This has been described in horrifying detail by historian Ronald Hamowy in "The IRS and Civil Liberties: Powers of Search and Seizure," on which the summary that follows is based.[35]

Hamowy begins by noting that "the protections afforded each American from arbitrary government action are nowhere more attenuated than in the case of enforcement of the tax laws."[36] The core of the problem, as suggested above, is that the information the IRS needs to carry out its mandate originates in private, peaceful income-producing exchanges between consenting persons. They are expected to report the fruit of those activities to the IRS, which is why the authorities like to claim the system is "voluntary." But the authorities also know that people prefer to keep their income rather than to give it to the government. So Congress and the courts have reasoned that if the IRS is to do its job, it must have mechanisms for obtaining personal information that no other agency of government needs or has. That explains the disparity in powers between the IRS and every other agency.

The laws require taxpayers to keep records about their financial activities, without specifying the form those records must take. The IRS can demand and use those records against a taxpayer. Thus, as already noted, the Constitution's Fifth Amendment protection against self-incrimination, which applies throughout the criminal law, does not exist in the tax law. Of course, the lack of records can also be used against the taxpayer. For example, if the IRS assesses a taxpayer's net worth as part of a prosecution, the taxpayer has an unpleasant choice. Should he submit a net-worth statement, he'd better have records documenting every part of his financial history. Incomplete records leave him at the mercy of the IRS. But if he chooses not to submit a statement, he is equally at the mercy of the agency, since the IRS is presumed to be correct in its assessment. The taxpayer would have no way to rebut the IRS's claims about his tax liability.

There was a time in American history when such power evoked revulsion. In 1885, the landmark case *Boyd v. United States* prompted a Supreme Court justice to write that "any compulsory discovery by extorting the party's oath, or compelling the production of his private books and papers, to convict him of a crime, or to forfeit his property, is contrary to the principles of a free government.... It may suit the purposes of a despotic power; but it cannot abide the pure atmosphere of political liberty and personal freedom."[37]

It is different today. The IRS's broad power covers not only the taxpayer but anyone else who possesses his records or other information deemed relevant — however remote. If an IRS agent issues a summons for records, it could be a criminal violation to refuse to produce them, punishable by a $1,000 fine and up to a year in prison. Before 1964, the IRS could simply arrest a person who refused to comply with a summons. The law has since been changed so that the IRS has to ask the court to hold him in contempt. That allows the subject to appear at a hearing while not under arrest.

The point of limited government is to restrict power in order to protect the rights and privacy of the people. In the United States one might expect some severe limits on what the IRS can do in investigating the taxpayers. But Hamowy found that "for the most part, the powers of the IRS are bounded by no effective restrictions, not even by that afforded by the constitutional guarantee against unreasonable searches and seizures." He also notes that "in the area of federal tax law, individual rights, in practice, do not take precedence over administrative authority."[38]

Paper Restrictions

Even the few restrictions written into the law turn out to be barely any restriction at all. Again, the government's need for revenue takes precedence even over the letter of the law. For example, the IRS's authority to examine records appears to be limited to "relevant" materials. Under the rule of law, the government is not supposed to be able to indiscriminately demand a citizen's private papers and then go hunting for crimes. A tax agent's summons for records, like a normal search warrant, is supposed to reasonably describe what is sought. But the courts have interpreted that restriction practically out of existence. A summons, say the courts, need not describe the documents sought in detail; it need only specify enough information to permit the taxpayer or other custodian of the records to identify them. And what is "relevant" has been held to include records that "might throw light" on the accuracy of a tax return. The courts have also said that it is not within their province to judge whether a tax investigation is proper. That's the IRS's business alone. Their concern is "only whether the documents sought are reasonably likely to relate to such an investigation."[39]

This means that if the IRS follows a few guidelines, it may engage in fishing expeditions with the taxpayers' records. Indeed, the courts have said that "some exploration or fishing necessarily is inherent and entitled to exist in all documentary productions."[40]

That sounds like a blank check. The court's interpretation of the law comes down to this: if the IRS is deemed to have issued its summons for records in good faith and not for the purpose of harassment, it can see virtually any records it wishes. The courts, the traditional bulwark between the citizen and the state, will not interfere. If the taxpayer believes the IRS did not act in good faith, the burden of proof is his.

As noted, another area where the IRS has unprecedented powers arises out of its authority to bring both criminal and civil cases. Under the protections of the Fourth and Fifth Amendments (prohibiting unreasonable searches and seizures, and forced self-incrimination), the IRS should not be able to summon records in a criminal investigation. But what if a civil case, where those protections don't apply, turns into a criminal case at some point? The same taxpayer conduct can bring both civil and criminal charges. At first the courts said that a civil summons could not be used to amass evidence for a criminal case. Such a use of the summons, a court ruled in 1953, would "diminish one of the fundamental guarantees of liberty."[41] But a later court rejected that reasoning and ruled that the mere possibility of a criminal proceeding did not make use of the summons improper. Another federal court upheld the summons even though it was aware that the IRS advised agents to keep quiet about the criminal investigation in order to induce self-incrimination. Later, the U.S. Supreme Court, in the 1971 case *Donaldson v. United States*, approved the so-called dual-purpose summons as long as it is issued in good faith and before a recommendation for criminal prosecution.

That rule was weak enough. But it got weaker. In 1978, the U.S. Supreme Court, ruling in *United States v. LaSalle National Bank*, reversed the circuit court of appeals and said that the good-faith requirement, as Hamowy summarized it, "is to be understood as having reference not to the statements or acts of any single agent but by an examination of the institutional posture of the IRS itself"![42] In other words, bad faith has to be imputable to the whole agency or its policies. That of course would be impossible to prove to a court's satisfaction. How would a taxpayer gather evidence for such a charge?

Another way that government power has traditionally been limited is through the doctrine of the statute of limitations. That doctrine forces the government to bring a criminal case within a specified period in order to prevent it from harassing citizens by indefinitely threatening them with prosecution. The IRS faces a statute of limitations also, at least on paper. The Internal Revenue Code states that tax deficiencies must be assessed within three years of the filing of the return. The courts have taken this to mean that the IRS may not summon older records.

But the IRS has a variety of ways to get around that restriction. It is allowed, for instance, to examine older records if it claims they relate to a year within the allowable period. The agency has been permitted to go back as far as thirty years under that reasoning.

The IRS is also allowed an exemption to the statute of limitations if it suspects fraud. There has been much legal wrangling over what the IRS must do to show fraud for this purpose, and the courts have come down squarely on the agency's side. A tax agent merely has to tell the court he has reason to suspect fraud in order to have access to records that otherwise would be beyond the allowable period. He need not show anything — not even probable cause. For

Hamowy, "The Court's position thus effectively destroyed any protection afforded a taxpayer from demands to produce his books and records by the statute of limitations.... [The IRS] may investigate capriciously and at its whim any period in the taxpayer's history, thus making the statute of limitations meaningless."[43]

The IRS also has administrative procedures that enable it to get around the statute of limitations. There is no rest for the weary taxpayer.

That pattern is repeated in many other areas of tax law. A restriction appears on the books. But administrative procedures and court interpretations nullify them. Restrictions can be set aside if the IRS believes tax collection is in jeopardy.[44] The constitutional prohibition against unreasonable searches and seizures has few teeth when applied to the IRS. Apparently it is impossible for the Internal Revenue Service to act unreasonably. It can demand virtually anything it wants. It has been permitted, for example, to look at patients' hospital records in order to investigate a doctor who was suspected of understating his income.[45] Moreover, a taxpayer has no standing to make a Fourth Amendment challenge to a summons issued to a third party, such as a bank. Citizens, in other words, cannot look to their banks, or anyone else, for financial privacy. (The Orwellian Bank Secrecy Act essentially forbids bank secrecy.) James Payne calculated that third parties must report eighty-one types of personal information to the IRS.[46]

It gets worse. By law, the IRS is supposed to inform a taxpayer that his bank has been ordered to turn over records. That requirement is intended to permit the taxpayer to intervene and perhaps block compliance. But the IRS can circumvent the notification requirement by informally requesting records. Banks usually cooperate with the IRS — they can be intimidated too. The courts have okayed this obvious strategy to avoid having to notify taxpayers.[47]

The courts have also ruled that, for Fourth Amendment purposes, a taxpayer does not have an expectation of privacy when he turns his financial records over to an accountant. There is no accountant-client privilege. (As we have already seen with the doctor-patient privilege, the attorney-client privilege also can be breached under some circumstances.[48])

On rare occasions, the IRS has been found to have illegally seized records. But it would be an error to conclude that the agency was therefore barred from using information that was improperly obtained. Unlike the normal criminal proceeding, where Fourth Amendment violations lead to suppression of evidence, in the tax arena, the evidence may be used to develop other evidence against the taxpayer. A finding of an illegal search has almost no consequences. "This ability to use evidence against a taxpayer that had been discovered through leads provided by illegally seized evidence provides a particularly potent weapon to the IRS," Hamowy writes.[49]

Despite court declarations to the contrary, it is hard to square the vast powers of the IRS with the Bill of Rights, which is supposedly still cherished in the United States. There was a time when a man's home was his castle. But that time ended when the taxation of incomes was permitted and the IRS was established by the U.S. Congress. Comparing the IRS's investigative authority to that of the Star Chamber, Hamowy writes, "It is only a slight exaggeration to say that, in tax cases, the constitutional safeguard against unreasonable searches and seizures is attenuated to the point where it has no bearing on the activities of the IRS."[50]

It would be wrong to think that the evils described here could be ended by enacting a better Taxpayers' Bill of Rights, by putting better people in office, or by setting up stern congressional watchdog commissions. That would change very little, but it might produce a false sense of security. The abuse of taxpayers flows logically and inexorably from what the IRS was set up to accomplish: the collection of taxes on income. In a sense, it is not the IRS's fault. As long as income is taxed, some government agency will be empowered to do the kinds of things that the IRS does today. The way to eliminate the evil of the IRS is to eliminate the evil of the income tax and the Sixteenth Amendment. Then, and only then, can the proper political relationship between citizen and state be restored.

In the chapter that follows we will look at how the income tax makes our whole society less prosperous.

Notes

¹ James L. Payne, *Costly Returns: The Burdens of the U.S. Tax System* (San Francisco: ICS Press, 1993), pp. 137–38, 163–78.

² Ibid., pp. 171–72.

³ Quoted in ibid., p. 70.

⁴ David Burnham, *A Law Unto Itself: Power, Politics and the IRS* (New York: Random House, 1989), p. 16.

⁵ Daniel J. Pilla, "Why You Can't Trust the IRS," Cato Institute Policy Analysis no. 222, April 15, 1995, at www.cato.org.

⁶ Burnham, p. 19.

⁷ Ibid., p. 21.

⁸ Ibid., p. 69.

⁹ Quoted in Charles Adams, *For Good and Evil: The Impact of Taxes on the Course of Civilization* (Lanham, Md.: Madison Books, 1993), pp. 385, 389.

¹⁰ Frank Chodorov, *The Income Tax: Root of All Evil* (New York: Devin-Adair, 1954), p. 65.

¹¹ The IRS mission — depriving people of their property — is corrupt per se. But for documentation of conventional corruption — bribe-taking, et cetera — at the agency, see Burnham, pp. 167–98. Chodorov comments, "It is now part of the American folklore that agents of the Internal Revenue Bureau [as it was once called] have been amenable to bribery, that 'pull' has played a part in the adjustment of disputed tax returns, that cases against tax dodgers have been quashed by higher-ups after field agents have conscientiously worked them up" (p. 64). He adds that this ability to directly influence the IRS is available only to the well-off.

¹² Burnham, pp. 255–90. Burnham was specifically referring to political and social activities and IRS control via the granting and withholding of tax-exempt status. But the power of the IRS goes beyond those areas and into the economic.

¹³ George Lardner Jr., "Nixon Sought 'Ruthless' Chief," *Washington Post*, January 3, 1997, p. A1.

¹⁴ Burnham documents such abuses extensively in *A Law Unto Itself*, pp. 226–54. See also Pilla. Revelations continue to be made. See Tom Rhodes, "Kennedys Put Tax Squeeze on Foes," *Times of London*, January 29, 1997 (Internet ed.). In a recent letter, Burnham wrote, "It appears, in fact, that President Franklin Roosevelt may have been the champion abuser" (*Washington Post*, Letter to the

editor, January 26, 1997, p. C6).

[15] As this book was being completed it was revealed that in fiscal 1994 and 1995 there were more than 1,500 cases of IRS employees' misusing tax records. That is nothing new. See Stephen Barr, "IRS Audit Reveals More Tax Browsing," *Washington Post*, April 9, 1997, p. A1."

[16] Burnham, p. 16.

[17] Ibid., p. 45.

[18] Ibid., p. 44. See also Pilla.

[19] James Bovard, *Lost Rights: The Destruction of American Liberty* (New York: St. Martin's Griffin, 1995), p. 270. See also Burnham, pp. 111–39, and Payne, pp. 50–52, 73–74.

[20] Burnham, p. 60.

[21] Ibid., p. 165.

[22] Payne, p. 80. See also Martin L. Gross, "Taxpayer's Rights: Almost None," in *The Tax Racket: Government Extortion from A to Z* (New York: Ballantine Books, 1995), pp. 240–50. Gross writes that the bill has been of some "limited value" to taxpayers but was quickly seen as inadequate (p. 247).

[23] Burnham, p. 310. Burnham adds that some members of Congress who might otherwise like to extend more legal rights to taxpayers fear angering the IRS (p. 303). Gross notes that a 1995 bill introduced by Rep. James Traficant, which would have shifted the burden of proof to the IRS, was buried in a House subcommittee (pp. 240–42).

[24] Gross, p. 248.

[25] "Nation's Largest Taxpayer Group Praises Taxpayer Rights Bill, Urges More IRS Curbs," National Taxpayers Union News Release, July 25, 1996, p. 2. The bill also gives taxpayers more scope to sue the IRS when it has been "reckless" and allows taxpayers who prevail against the IRS to recover more civil damages and attorney's fees than previously.

[26] Albert B. Crenshaw, "With Little Opposition or Debate, House Passes Bill That Would Overhaul IRS," *Washington Post*, November 6, 1997, p. A14.

[27] Burnham, pp. 141, 153. Quotas were formally outlawed in 1988, but Bovard says there is evidence they may continue informally (p. 269).

[28] Bovard, pp. 268–69.

[29] Ibid., pp. 266, 270.

[30] Payne, pp. 73–74.

[31] Ibid., pp. 71–72.

[32] Bovard, p. 281.

[33] Ibid., p. 283.

[34] Shelley L. Davis, "The IRS Out of Control," *Wall Street Journal*, April 15, 1996, editorial page. Also see "Why the IRS Is the Government's Most Secretive Agency," *Chronicle of Higher Education*, March 15, 1996, and *Unbridled Power: Inside the Secret Culture of the IRS* (New York: HarperCollins, 1997), both by Shelley Davis.

[35] Ronald Hamowy, "The IRS and Civil Liberties: Powers of Search and Seizure," *Cato Journal* 1 (Spring 1981): 225–75.

[36] Ibid., p. 225.

[37] Quoted in Adams, p. 388.

[38] Hamowy, p. 233.

[39] Ibid. p. 233. The quote is from the 1959 case *United States v. First National Bank of Fort Smith.*

[40] Quoted in ibid., p. 260, from *Schwimmer v. United States*, a 1956 circuit court case.

[41] Ibid., p. 235. The case was *United States v. O'Connor.*

[42] Ibid., p. 238.

[43] Ibid., p. 241.

[44] See Payne, p. 246, note 8.

[45] Hamowy, p. 244.

[46] Payne, p. 137.

[47] Hamowy, pp. 249–50.

[48] See Payne, pp. 137, and 246, note 14.

[49] Hamowy, p. 252.

[50] Ibid., p. 253.

4

The Income Tax Makes
You Poorer

Whave seen how the income tax and all that follows logically
from it offend the moral sense on which this nation was founded
and subjugate people to the state. That in itself is enough to con-
demn it. But the harm does not stop there. The income tax is destructive in material terms. Because of that tax, you are likely to be
poorer than you would otherwise be.

Society in general is poorer because, to use the distinction
made by James Payne, of a double whammy: the tax burden and the
tax-system burden.[1] The money extracted by the income tax is, of
course, money that cannot be consumed or invested to create prosperity. That is a huge cost. But beyond that, the system itself imposes a huge cost. Its arcane rules discourage productive enterprise.
The system induces people to make decisions for tax purposes that
they otherwise would not have made. It forces people to spend time
and money complying with laws that change frequently. It creates
uncertainty about the future. It imposes stress, as people wonder
whether they have run afoul of the law. All of that represents a loss
of well-being to people and their society. Payne conservatively estimates that those costs (in 1990 terms) come to more than $500
billion each year, or 65 percent of the money raised by the system.
Many of the costs have gone up in the years since.[2]

The Market Process

To understand the complete burden, let us look briefly at a

market economy unencumbered by an income tax. In the market-place, people working under a division of labor produce and trade products and services, including labor. When people produce more than they consume, they save and invest. Rising living standards depend on savings and investment, which increase productivity and raise wages. Entrepreneurs, looking to earn profits, accumulate or borrow savings, which they use to purchase the labor and other resources required to make the things people will want to buy. The competitive market process results from the absence of legal barriers to production and exchange, in other words, from the protection of property rights.

The price system, which is generated ultimately by the buying and selling decisions of consumers, communicates information to all market participants about what should be produced. The system is particularly important for indicating to entrepreneurs where errors have been made in allocating resources among various consumer needs. If an entrepreneur makes a profit, that is a sign that the purpose to which he channeled labor and other resources was worthwhile in the eyes of consumers. The threat of losses is his reality check.

To highlight some key points about the market process: People earn income and profits through voluntary exchange for mutual benefit. In the market, all a producer can do is offer something at attractive terms. It is up to others to accept or decline the offer. Businessmen therefore must strive to serve the interests of potential customers. (In describing the workings of the market, it is immaterial that their motive is self-interest. Insofar as they seek income, they must look after the desires of consumers.)

We conclude then that when someone prospers in a market, it is a sign he has catered well to the wants and tastes of consumers. (He may be making things far removed from the retail level. But those things must contribute to the creation of valued consumer products or else his efforts will have no market value.) To put it another way, high incomes do not come at the expense of others generally. What is received as income is voluntarily given in exchange for something the buyer values more. Income is the reward for supplying something that people want. A high income is the reward for extraordinary foresight or ability. In a market economy disparities in incomes do not indicate that something is awry. They are a gauge of differences in the ability to serve consumers. People differ in that ability. Therefore incomes differ. It should be added here that the market offers no guarantees. Someone who is successful this year could fail next year. The Fortune 500 list in 1997 is different from the list in 1957 and 1977. Consumers can be fickle; they don't care about past service. To become fixated on income levels and disparities, one must forget that people are constantly moving up and down the ladder. What counts is the lack of barriers to mobility, not disparity. The market economy permits mobility.

Another important thing to grasp is that although people with high incomes can enjoy high levels of consumption, they save more than others. They can afford to. But they don't stuff the money in their mattresses. They invest it, and that investment benefits the entire society by bringing better and less-expensive products and services to the rest of us. In a market economy high-income people are led to raise everyone's living standards, to quote Adam Smith, "as if by an invisible hand." In moral terms, high incomes need not be justified by "service" to society at large. The voluntary process that produced the incomes sufficiently justifies them. But in economic terms, it is critical to understand that high incomes benefit the larger society. Even when rich people consume by buying furs and yachts they create employment opportunities for the less well-off. Recall that when Congress passed a luxury tax a few years ago, the biggest victims were working people who lost jobs — and the tax was for that reason repealed.

The upshot is that high incomes are an unmitigated blessing for society. They provide the incentives and resources for people to produce the things that make our lives better. A tax policy based on the idea that high incomes or income differences are maladies to be eliminated is a policy that will hurt the very people who are thought to need help.

The Income Tax Lowers Living Standards

It should be clear how the introduction of an income tax into the market process must depress the production of prosperity. (The same can be said for other kinds of taxes, of course.) Whether flat or progressive, an income tax takes increasing amounts of money from people as their incomes rise. Less money is left for savings and investment. The natural progress of the market toward higher living standards is thus stifled.

Income taxation transfers purchasing power to the government. By spending the revenue, of course, government transfers the wealth to others, a vast array of suppliers, welfare recipients, government employees, consultants, and so on. The people who produced the wealth cannot use it according to their preferences. People who

53

did not produce the wealth are empowered to spend it according to theirs. The tax diverts the market process from the path it would have followed without the tax. No matter how it is imposed, it will rearrange resources. The market's function of serving consumers is undermined because through the tax the government and its clients in part determine what is produced. Investment decisions are affected by what the government buys and whom it finances. Without the tax, the market carries out the wishes of consumers as anticipated by entrepreneurs. Consumers might have spent their money on televisions and compact discs. Or their savings might have gone to produce new things altogether. But the tax instead diverts their wealth to producers of, say, missiles, airplanes, military uniforms, spacecraft, paper clips, and whatever else the government buys. That leaves fewer scarce resources for what consumers want.

Taxation, the late economist Murray Rothbard wrote, separates production from distribution. In the free market, production and "distribution" are two aspects of a single phenomenon. To be precise, in the market income wealth is not distributed; it is produced and exchanged. But as soon as taxation is introduced, there is a new factor: the allocation of the wealth extracted.[3] Taxation creates two classes that do not exist without it: tax producers (payers) and tax consumers. Taxpayers are the creators of wealth. Tax consumers are those who receive some or all of their income from tax revenues. Rothbard, drawing on the Southern statesman John C. Calhoun, emphasized the implications that this class division has for society, particularly how it undermines social harmony by creating a conflict of interest among the two groups.

Most discussion of taxation assumes that the people at large benefit from government spending and that the benefits outweigh the costs of taxation. One of the few political economists to question that assumption was the Frenchman J.-B. Say in the early nineteenth century. In his classic work, *A Treatise on Political Economy*, Say discussed taxation in the chapter titled "On Consumption." Taxation is not usually thought of as a consumption activity. But for Say, taxation and government spending are not investments by the state. They are, indeed, acts of consumption. He said a tax is imposed "by the ruling power ... for the purpose of supplying the consumption it may think proper."[4] And in Say's view, "It makes a vast difference to the public prosperity, whether the individual or the state be the consumer."[5] He called the claim that taxes are payments for services "a gross fallacy [because] the value paid to government by the tax-payer is given without equivalent or return."[6]

According to Rothbard, calling government spending "consumption" is entirely justified because through taxation government officials substitute their preferences for the preferences of those who produced the wealth. Government "investment" is not driven, as market investment is, by the choices of consumers, but by those of politicians, bureaucrats, and their clients. "Once let the tax be eliminated, and the producers are free to earn and consume. The new investments called forth by the demands of the specially privileged will turn out to be *malinvestments*."[7] Say would have agreed. He pointed out that the diversion of capital from private to government purposes reduces the well-being of society, "for industry may be presumed to have chosen the most profitable channel."[8] In other words, entrepreneurs seeking profit are better at satisfying the needs of people than bureaucrats. They have a stronger incentive to be so, and they have the best reality check known: the profit and loss system. Businessmen who fail to satisfy consumers lose access to capital; those who succeed earn profits. Government programs tend to work in the reverse. Bureaucrats have no incentive to serve the people at large (special interests dominate), although all are made to pay. Moreover, a government program is likely to receive more money if it fails to accomplish its goals.

Say insisted that taxation depresses production. "The subtraction of a product must needs diminish, instead of augmenting, productive power," he wrote. "It is a glaring absurdity to pretend that taxation contributes to national wealth by engrossing part of the national produce, and enriches the nation by consuming part of its wealth."[9] Implicit in Say's discussion is the view that anything worthwhile the government now does could be accomplished more efficiently without taxation.[10]

To appreciate how income taxation reduces prosperity from what it could be, imagine a 100 percent tax on incomes. We wouldn't expect much prosperity in such a society. People would have no incentive to earn money. They would devote resources to hiding the little they did earn. No investments would be made. No savings would exist to increase living standards. People's activities would be grossly influenced by the tax.

If we lower the rate from 100 percent, the principle does not change. The reduction merely lessens the effects of the tax. Other things being equal, the degree of prosperity in a society laboring under an income tax must be less than in a society without an income tax. If you want less of something, tax it.

We saw in chapter 2 the results of that principle. In the discussion of fairness, it was noted that when the top marginal tax rate is lowered, the top filers produce more wealth and then pay a greater portion of revenues than previously. The top marginal rates are indeed a disincentive for the people in the best position to invest. The principle is also illustrated by the fact that the share collected from the top 1 percent shrank after President Clinton raised the highest rate from 31 percent (where President Bush had pushed it) to 39.6 percent.[11] When the disincentive to produce is increased, those with resources turn to leisure. They lose out, but so does the rest of society. Lost production through taxation harms everyone.

An income tax must lower living standards. The tax reduces the compensation from work and investment and tampers with the natural incentives of the marketplace. That could have different effects on different people, but either way, their standards of living will be diminished. The tax on work could make leisure appear more attractive. If so, fewer tradable goods would be produced, making everyone poorer. But the loss of income might prompt some people to work more hours and give up leisure. The choice will depend on the subjective preferences of individuals. What matters is that the allocation of time between work and leisure has been upset by the government's forced extraction of wealth. Whatever a given person chooses, he is worse off than if the tax had not been imposed. The person who gives up work for leisure because of the tax will miss out on consumption and savings (for future consumption) that he would have engaged in. The person who gives up leisure for work will miss out on the satisfaction his leisure would have brought. In each case, the person's first choice has to be shelved for a less-preferred option.

A flat-rate, proportional income tax generally diminishes ability to produce, save, and invest simply by reducing the pay-off from work and by siphoning off capital. The more you earn, the more you pay, although the percentage remains the same. A progressive income tax can magnify that malevolent effect.[12] As a person earns more income, the tax rate increases. Thus, a progressive rate is a system of increasing disincentives to produce wealth. The difference between the pretax and after-tax return widens as people earn more money. For example, if at some level of income the tax rate jumps from 15 percent to 25 percent, an earner will have to calculate whether the extra effort required to raise his income is worth only 75 percent of the nominal return. He may decide it is not. That issue is more obvious at high levels of income when the rate structure is deeply progressive and the top rate is 70 percent to 90 percent, as it was in the United States between World War II and 1970. But the effect exists in diminished form at lower levels also.

Taxes on capital gains and corporate profits similarly create disincentives to produce. Since they reduce the return on investment, those taxes must affect investment decisions adversely for general economic well-being. The taxation of capital gains has other effects. By lowering the return on the sale of stock and other assets, the tax encourages people who own those things to hold on to them longer than they would have. Such tax-driven decisions reduce investment in new enterprises that would benefit millions of people. Taxation of capital gains thus makes the market process rigid and undermines it. Moreover, in times of inflation, investors pay on illusory gains because the tax is not indexed. Actual losses may be taxed because inflation makes them appear to be gains. It is no accident that (other things being equal) nations that have lower capital gains taxes, or none at all, have a greater rate of savings and domestic investment and more robust economic growth.[13]

Incidentally, defenders of the capital gains tax portray it as a tax on the rich. Even if that were so, it would not be a good reason to keep the tax. The rich have rights too. But in fact, it is not correct. The Tax Foundation has revealed that from 1942 to 1992, about a third of the capital gains tax was paid by people making less than $100,000.[14]

Another way that the income tax does harm is through the double taxation on savings. Money saved is taxed the same as money put toward consumption; so is the resulting interest income. That would seem on the surface to be even-handed treatment of all income. But actually it is not. The paradox is resolved by realizing that savings and consumption have an important difference: the time dimension. People save in order to consume more (thanks to interest) in the future, and that fact has important tax implications.

Imagine that someone is deciding what to with $1,000 just earned. That person will compare the satisfaction he can obtain from direct consumption, say, buying a big-screen television, with the future income that could be generated by investing the money in a CD at the bank. The $1,000 is taxed at the relevant rate whether the money is consumed or saved. Our earner will have to buy a smaller television or save less than would be possible if the tax didn't exist. But the tax will reduce the investment a *second time*, because the interest on the CD will also be taxed. In other words, the returns on consumption, being nonmaterial, are not taxed. But the returns on savings are. In that way, the income tax penalizes investment more heavily than consumption.[15]

The implications for decision-making and economic progress are significant. The National Commission on Economic Growth and Taxation said that because the income tax reduces the return from investment "saving and investment must earn substantially higher returns to cover the added taxes and still be worthwhile substitutes for consumption…. The current biases in the tax treatment of capital have cost the economy several trillion dollars in savings and investment, considerably retarding the growth of productivity, wages, and employment, and retarding the growth of individual income and wealth. It is no exaggeration to suggest that the level of income in the United States could be at least 15 to 20 percent higher than it is today if these biases did not exist."[16]

A chronic complaint about America is that the savings rate is too low. It is often pointed out that nations (such as some in Asia) that do not tax savings, or that tax them at a lower rate, have higher savings rates. That is to be expected. But some comments are in order. There is no special vice in taxing savings versus consumption. Taxing either one diminishes well-being. People allocate their income between consumption and savings on the basis of their subjective preferences. Their decisions should rule. The proper aggregate savings rate is the one that emerges from the free decisions of all market participants. What is wrong with taxation is that it interferes with those decisions, not that it burdens savers. Champions of liberty and consumer sovereignty should not imply that it is better to tax consumption than savings, for that suggests that it is more virtuous to save than consume. What if a free people saves "too little"? Should there be a government program to induce people to save more? Government is best kept out of private decision-making.[17]

The upshot is that the government should stop discouraging savings. But that is different from saying that it should encourage it.[18]

The penalties and disincentives of the income tax obviously take their greatest toll on those who have little wealth now. The tax is inherently tougher on people trying to accumulate wealth as opposed to those who already have done so. Although in 1986 many low-income people were dropped off the tax rolls, that obstacle is not entirely gone from the system. Moreover, as already indicated, the tax on high-income savers and investors hurts low-income people, who are deprived of new opportunities and products. Consider the crazy logic of the welfare state. Government subjects people to grueling taxes, which especially impede lower-income people from climbing to a higher living standard. Then it throws them bones in the form of subsidies. If the policymakers really cared about lower-income people and understood even a smidgen of economics, they would get rid of all income taxes and subsidies. That would be the best way to help people climb the economic ladder.

Manipulation via the Tax Code

The people who write tax legislation are aware of the disincentives involved in progressive taxation, and they have tried to mitigate those effects without giving up progressivity altogether. That has resulted in the crazy-quilt system of tax deductions and credits that so many people complain about. It should be pointed out that most of these preferences benefit those who are better off. First, they more often apply to the activities of the better-off. Second, expensive tax advice, which most middle-class and working-class people can't afford, may be needed to take advantage of them. Finally, deductions are worth more in the higher tax brackets.

Given the objections to progressivity, the lowering of the real tax rate through deductions and credits may seem like a blessing. But they bring their own problems. The methods used to offset the system's disincentives influence people's behavior, undermine the efficacy of the marketplace, and increase the burden of the tax process. That is because the preferences target particular activities chosen arbitrarily through the political system.

To the extent that economic activity is directed by the tax-bill writers and the people who influence them, the market process is less capable of serving the public than it would otherwise be. If a deduction is allowed for activity X but not activity Y, people will tend to pursue activity X. The people who write the tax code may think activity X is more worthy than activity Y, but that could be an arbitrary decision. And even if it is not strictly arbitrary, their decision is presumptuous, for it interferes with the free decision-making of market participants. Besides, if X were really more worthwhile, it would be chosen without government encouragement. In a free market, consumers determine what investment activities are undertaken in the market because serving consumers is how entrepreneurs earn profits. When the tax code distracts entrepreneurs from that task, society is worse off. The code's jungle of technical rules regarding deductions, allowances, depreciation schedules, and the rest (all of which would be abolished along with the income tax) is a massive intrusion into the entrepreneurial process. Instead of concentrating on how best to increase people's living standards, businessmen must be concerned with minimizing the taxes they have to pay. Taxes reduce the returns to investment, of course, and thus make some worthy projects uneconomical. Moreover, to minimize taxes, entrepreneurs may have to do wasteful things that reduce prosperity. That is most obvious with tax shelters, in which people can cut their taxes by engaging in explicitly unproductive activities. Although tax-law changes have made most tax shelters passé, that aspect of the code is not gone entirely. For example, since the interest on municipal bonds is tax-free, money that would have gone toward satisfying consumer preferences instead is dedicated to local projects.

We should not underestimate how manipulative the government can be through the tax code. Depending on how it treats real-estate investments, the government can, and has, set off booms and busts, creating and then wiping out fortunes. The infamous S&L crisis was precipitated in part by a change in the tax rules for real estate in 1986. A seemingly small tax change can destroy someone's business plans and profits. Or it can make someone else a millionaire. Imagine the potential for corruption.

A perfect example of how tax preferences distort decision-making is the exemption of employer-provided medical insurance from taxation. People ordinarily would prefer cash to benefits. But since cash compensation is taxed and insurance is not, workers have an incentive to accept more of their pay in the form of insurance. As a result, people most likely use medical insurance to a far greater extent than otherwise — even for small, routine expenses. Because of the overhead, first-dollar medical coverage would probably be a bad buy. (People don't buy such coverage for their automobiles.) But the perception that medical services paid by insurance companies are free (or close to it) encourages consumers to be complacent about price. They unwittingly bid up the price of services and in turn the price of insurance. The government then uses price inflation as a pretext for taking over the health care industry.[19]

The problem is not that the government exempts medical benefits from the income tax. The problem is that it applies the tax to everything else. Note that a leading policy response to the distortion from the medical-insurance exemption is tax-free medical savings accounts. While MSAs expand the tax exemption, they also maintain the distortion on behalf of medical spending, since the money can only be used that way. Far better to abolish the tax and the preferences, letting consumers and investors make their decisions without government manipulation.

Because changes in the tax code can create opportunities for higher incomes, special interests spend a great deal of time lobbying the tax-writing committees for favorable changes. That is one reason the code changes so often. The process is hardly a search for the tax code that will best serve the public. Rather, it is a process in which special interests lobby their political friends for favors. And congressmen, always with an eye on the next election and in need of campaign donations, are eager to please people who can deliver money and votes.

Who's left out? Average taxpayers, of course. They are too busy raising their families and making a living to become informed about arcane tax-law changes, let alone to go to Washington, D.C., to lobby against them. Naturally, the changes tend to benefit small, well-organized groups and harm the vast majority of citizens.[20]

For the public-choice school of political economy, this is known as the problem of "dispersed costs" and "concentrated benefits." The cost of any particular tax change will be spread thin over the majority of citizens, making the burden on any individual small. Even if an individual understood what was happening (a big "if," given how technical and invisible the tax-legislation process is), he would have too small a monetary incentive to fight the change. In contrast, the benefits of the change are concentrated on a small special-interest group. The value to any individual member is large. He has a strong incentive to be informed about such issues and to support lobbying activities, perhaps through a trade association in Washington. Tax-law writing tends to be done by a closed clique of congressmen, tax officials, and special interests. The average taxpayer doesn't stand a chance under those circumstances.

Manipulation through tax policy is getting more popular with lawmakers all the time. They love to say, if you do X, you can keep your money. If you do anything else, you cannot. President Clinton says just that when he proposes tax relief consisting of deductions for only certain kinds of spending, say, buying a home or paying college tuition.

That is Big Brother in its subtle mode. Since people have become more skeptical about big government, it has been harder for politicians to launch big spending programs. So they have turned to another way of accomplishing their ends: manipulation through the tax code. Instead of openly subsidizing college tuition, President Clinton calls instead for a tax deduction or credit. He can achieve the same effect without a spending program. It is true that a deduction is not the same thing as a cash subsidy. But manipulation of behavior occurs in both cases. Better to abolish the income tax and let people make their own decisions with their own money.

Politicians like these gimmicks at election time, and voters may thrill to talk about "tax relief." But tax relief through deductions is very precarious. It is a way for the government to let you keep a little cash without conceding that it is your money. Tax deductions can be taken away (though some, like the mortgage-interest deduction, are harder to take than others). The courts, naturally, do not see tax deductions as a return of stolen property to the taxpayers. "An income tax deduction is a matter of legislative grace," the U.S. Supreme Court said in 1943.[21] In other words, all income belongs to the state. If it allows you to use some of it for purposes it chooses, be grateful. But don't think it is yours as a matter of right. That is where the Sixteenth Amendment to the U.S. Constitution has delivered us.

To repeat, it is not exemptions from income taxation that need to be abolished but income taxation itself.

The Burden of Uncertainty

A fluid tax code is a bad thing. No one can say what will be in the code from year to year. Sometimes the changes are even retroactive. As noted earlier, the tax code was changed more than one hundred times in the 1980s alone. The "simplification" of the 1986 Tax Reform Act amended two thousand sections. One hundred new forms were introduced.[22] The changes continued in the 1990s with President Bush's and President Clinton's tax-rate increases. A tax exemption people count on one year can be gone the next. Who can confidently make long-term plans when a tax amendment next year or in ten years could drastically change conditions and reduce the anticipated return? This is not to say that long-term planning does not occur in the U.S. economy. But since the uncertainty of the tax code is a way of life, investment and other planning is surely less ambitious than it would be without the income tax. It would be naive to think that the ever-present threat of amendment does not affect how entrepreneurs act. Economists Alan Auerbach and James Hines have said that "in the uncertain business of planning for U.S. corporate investment, one of the few reliable forecasts one can make is that the tax law will change before any new investment outlives its usefulness."[23]

James Payne asked an accountant who specializes in small

corporations how the tax code affects planning. The accountant replied, "Oh you can't plan. There is no way you can plan. You don't know what the tax law's going to be this year, let alone next. And they make things retroactive."[24]

Payne wished to quantify the full cost of tax uncertainty, but he found it impossible, since uncertainty is subjective. The closest he could come was an estimate of the cost that uncertainty about tax rates creates for work and savings decisions. Analyst Jonathan Skinner, using the period 1929–1975, estimated that "the annual loss of uncertain taxation, expressed as a proportion of 1985 U.S. national income, is $12 billion."[25] Payne suspects that is an underestimate because it accounted for changes in rates only and because the period looked at had fewer changes than subsequent periods. But the point is made: uncertainty about the tax code takes its toll on the capacity of the U.S. economy to create prosperity.

The cost of uncertainty is but one aspect of what Payne calls the burden of the tax *system*, which comes on top of the burden of the tax itself. Let's look now at other costs the system imposes on the American people. Payne catalogues and conservatively estimates the (1985) costs for individuals and businesses this way:

Compliance: $159.4 billion (computed on 5.424 billion hours plus the amount spent on paid preparers used by individuals)

Enforcement costs (audits, litigation, forced collections): $12.9 billion

Disincentives to production: $155.3 billion

Disincentives from tax uncertainty: $12 billion

Evasion and avoidance: $19.3 billion

Government operations: $4 billion

That totals $362.9 billion. Payne emphasizes that the various costs are hard to quantify and that those numbers are underestimates. He doesn't even try to attach numbers to the emotional, moral, and cultural burden of the tax system.

Small Business and the Self-Employed

The special burden of the tax system on small business and the self-employed should be emphasized. Large companies, of course, can afford the accounting and legal services that are required to grapple with the difficult and ever-changing tax code. Small-business owners and the self-employed often cannot. The record keeping, form filing, and need to be informed about the tax laws surely discourage a significant number of people from venturing into independent entrepreneurship. The system hampers the entrepreneurs who proceed anyway. That burden represents a loss to everyone, because small business is a major source of innovative products and services that raise our living standards. It is also a major source of jobs. Anything that stunts the development of small business is bad for our economic well-being. Imagine the additional prosperity the American people would enjoy if the income tax were lifted off the shoulders of small business.

The self-employed have another burden to carry: IRS animosity. It seems that the agency doesn't like people who work for themselves; taxes are easier to collect from people who have employers to do withholding. "The IRS has long striven to minimize the number of self-employed," writes James Bovard.[26] As a result of its efforts, thousands of small businesses have been damaged or disrupted in the health care and high-technology industries. The IRS has done that by classifying contractors as employees and penalizing companies that buy their services for not withholding taxes.[27]

The Growth of Government

The income tax opened the gates to the growth of the federal government. It is hard to imagine today's federal government supporting itself by excise taxes and tariffs, which were relied on before the income tax became a tax for ordinary people in World War II. Indeed, when the income tax became fashionable among America's intellectuals, they argued that the modern state requires access to new sources of revenue in order to do things that government did not have to do before. What they had in mind, of course, was the welfare state, which they had observed in Bismarck's Germany, and an activist foreign policy, under which the U.S. government would guarantee "American interests" all around the world. Those are expensive items. The source of revenue with the biggest potential pay-off was the new fortunes being made by industrialists, particularly in the northeastern United States. (See chapter 5.) That wealth looked like a huge ripe plum ready for picking. Since most people were not making those fortunes, there was little public opposition.

The income tax was not a big revenue producer at first because it hit only a small percentage of Americans. But thanks to two world wars, the tax became a revenue gusher. The individual income tax raised $420 million, or about 14 percent of all federal receipts, in 1934. In those days the budget was $6.5 billion (unadjusted dollars). In 1942, America's first full year in World War II, the tax brought in $3.3 billion, or 22 percent of receipts. In 1944 the take came to $19.7 billion — 44 percent of total receipts.

That demonstrated to the policymakers that the individual income tax was a bonanza indeed (as was the corporation income tax). The war ended in 1945, but the amount raised by the income tax never fell back by any significant amount. In 1951, the tax was raising more than it raised at its wartime height in 1944. It has been up and up ever since, with only a few minor exceptions. In fiscal year 1997, the tax was expected to raise $645 billion, or 43 percent — the biggest single source — of total federal receipts in a budget of more than $1.6 trillion.

We have understated the amount the government extracts, because we left out the payroll taxes that finance Social Security and Medicare, and the corporation income tax. All of these reduce incomes to some extent. When you add those revenues to the personal income tax, the total comes to $1.3 trillion for fiscal year 1997.

To put this all in perspective, the federal government, thanks to the Sixteenth Amendment and the income taxes it permits, has perpetrated the biggest hold-up in the history of the world. We have all paid the price in lost prosperity.

In the next chapter, we will see how the income tax came to the land of the free.

Notes

[1] James L. Payne, *Costly Returns: The Burdens of the U.S. Tax System* (San Francisco: ICS Press, 1993). This is apparently the only book that attempts a full accounting of the burdens of taxation in the United States.

[2] Ibid., p. 9.

[3] Murray N. Rothbard, *Power and Market: Government and the Economy* (Kansas City, Mo.: Sheed Andrews and McMeel, 1977), pp. 86–88.

[4] Jean-Baptiste Say, *A Treatise on Political Economy* (1803; New York: Augustus M. Kelley, 1971), p. 416.

[5] Quoted in Murray N. Rothbard, *Classical Economics: An Austrian Perspective on the History of Economic Thought*, vol. 2 (Brookfield, Vt.: Edward Elgar Publishing Co., 1995), p. 42.

[6] Ibid., p. 41.

[7] Rothbard, *Power and Market*, p. 98. Italics in original.

[8] Quoted in Rothbard, *Classical Economics*, p. 42.

[9] Say, p. 147.

[10] However, Say did not oppose all taxation, and even supported a progressive income tax.

[11] The numbers, which come from the Internal Revenue Service, are reported in Chris R. Edwards, "Who Pays Federal Income Taxes?" *Special Report* no. 42, November 1994, Tax Foundation. The 1994 numbers are at the foundation's website, www. taxfoundation.org/prtopincome.html.

[12] It should be acknowledged that, in theory, a progressive rate structure with low rates could be less damaging than a high flat rate.

[13] Stephen Moore and John Silvia, "The ABCs of the Capital Gains Tax," Cato Institute Policy Analysis no. 242, October 4, 1995. See also Martin L. Gross, "Capital Gains Tax: You Lose; Washington Wins — All the Time" in *The Tax Racket: Government Extortion from A to Z* (New York: Ballantine Books, 1995), pp. 52–58.

[14] "Who Earns Capital Gains, and Who Pays Capital Gains Taxes?" at the Tax Foundation website: www.taxfoundation.org/ prcapgains.html.

[15] This is drawn from Roy E. Cordato and Sheldon Richman, "A Tax Deduction for Education," *The Freeman*, June 1994, pp. 303–5.

[16] Stephen Entin, "Tax Biases Against Saving and Investment and How to Fix Them," in National Commission on Economic Growth and Tax Reform, *Unleashing America's Potential* (New York: St. Martin's Griffin, 1996), p. 69. Also see Laurence J. Kotlikoff, "The Economic Impact of Replacing Federal Income Taxes with a Sales Tax," Cato Policy Analysis no. 193, April 15, 1993.

[17] Rothbard concludes that even explicit consumption taxes must also tax savings implicitly because savings is motivated by future consumption. *Power and Market*, pp. 108–11.

[18] Ibid., p. 119–20. Congress, in its typically flawed way, tried to balance the disincentives by letting people create Individual Retirement Accounts. Deposits up to an arbitrary limit were tax-deferred until withdrawal at age 55 or later. Congress later added more restrictions, then reduced them.

[19] See John C. Goodman and Gerald L. Musgrave, *Patient Power: Solving America's Health Care Crisis* (Washington, D.C.: Cato Instute, 1992).

[20] See, for example, James Bovard, "Archer Daniels Midland: A Case Study in Corporate Welfare," Cato Institute Policy Analysis, no. 241, September 26, 1995.

[21] Quoted in James Bovard, *Lost Rights: The Destruction of American Liberty* (New York: St. Martin's Griffin, 1995), p. 291.

[22] Daniel J. Pilla, "Why You Can't Trust the IRS," Cato Institute Policy Analysis no. 222, April 15, 1995, at www.cato.org.

[23] Quoted in Payne, p. 96.

[24] Ibid., p. 97.

[25] Quoted in ibid., p. 98.

[26] Bovard, *Lost Rights*, p. 260. For details see pp. 259–65.

[27] See, for example, Jon Christensen, "Self-Employed under Fire by the IRS," *Wall Street Journal Interactive Edition*, June 6, 1996 (http://interactive.wsj.com) (editorial page).

5

How We Got the
Income Tax

In 1913 the Congress of the United States passed the income tax that has been with us ever since. That tax was enacted after the states ratified the Sixteenth Amendment to the U.S. Constitution:

> The Congress shall have power to lay and collect taxes on incomes, from whatever source derived, without apportionment among the several States, and without regard to any census or enumeration.

The tax enabled the federal government to amass unprecedented power over the lives and economic activities of the American people. It enabled the government to participate in global affairs and enter wars that would have been unthinkable without such a tax. In sum, it helped create the Leviathan that so many of the Founding Fathers feared might someday come to America and that plagues us to this day.

How did it happen? Why did a nation founded on the premise of minimum government and maximum individual freedom succumb to the political malady so characteristic of Europe, which the Founders had struggled so heroically to be free of?

It didn't happen overnight. The intellectual change in America that led to adoption of the income tax was a slow process working through many media. The process was fueled by several sources: populists envious of the wealth held by others, "Progressive" politicians seeking to consolidate power and to expand the functions of government, court intellectuals who foresaw the professional opportunities that big government would provide, and businessmen who understood that a well-funded, muscular state — not laissez faire — was the route to guaranteed success.

The first proposal for an income tax (and an inheritance tax) came during the War of 1812 against Britain. By 1814 the government had run up an unprecedented debt of $100 million. Most revenues were raised by customs duties on foreign products. Although they were doubled in 1812, they actually brought in less revenue because trade dropped off. By 1815 excise taxes had been imposed on domestic goods and commodities and taxes were put on houses, slaves, and land. All the new taxes were removed after the war, but a high protective tariff was passed in 1816 to retire the debt.[1]

The Civil War

The American people barely escaped an income tax during the war against Britain. They were not so lucky in the war between the states. The Civil War provided the rationale for Congress to pass six successive income-tax bills, setting a precedent that would dog the American people until the tax became a permanent fixture. The war of course was expensive — costing an average of $1.75 million a day.[2] Moreover, the South was no longer sending tariff revenues to Lincoln's government. To finance the Union effort, the Congress issued bonds and notes, doubled the tariff, sold public lands, imposed license fees, and increased old and created new excise taxes. None of this was enough.

In 1861 House Ways and Means Chairman Thaddeus Stevens, Republican of Pennsylvania, introduced a tax on land in each state "with each state's share to be apportioned by population."[3] The South and West objected because they felt they had already been stung by earlier tariffs on such basic things as tea, coffee, and sugar. Stevens countered by reducing the direct land tax and adding a tax on wealth and income. In July the House passed a 3 percent tax on all incomes over $600 a year. At the same time the Senate added to a tariff bill a 5 percent tax on all incomes over $1,000 a year. The conference committee compromised with a 3 percent tax on incomes over $600 ($10,500 in 1995 dollars). This was net income, with deductions to be specified by the Treasury. There was also to be a 1.5 percent tax on interest from government securities. The tax was due June 30, 1862, against 1861 incomes.

No money was ever raised by the income tax of 1862 because

a second tax passed before the first could take effect. In 1862 the war's demand on resources was immense, and bond sales were massive. In March the House passed a new revenue bill that included a tax similar to the first, but with a $600 exemption ($10,500 in 1995 dollars). The Senate made the rate progressive: 3 percent on incomes of $600 to $10,000; 5 percent on $10,000 to $50,000; and 7.5 percent over $50,000. Deductions were allowed for other taxes and for all profits or income "derived from ... any articles manufactured, upon which specific, stamp, or ad valorem duties shall have been directly assessed or paid...." This would have exempted most business income, but the provision was not used and a year later it was stricken.[4]

The conference committee compromised by eliminating the 7.5 percent rate. But it included a modest inheritance tax. The bill was signed by Lincoln on July 1, 1862, and it took effect a month later. It was to expire in 1866. By the time of passage the Union debt was $505 million.[5]

There were two interesting sidelights to the law. First, it included withholding of the tax on federal salaries and on interest and dividends, foreshadowing introduction of the withholding tax for everyone during World War II. Second, a year after the law was enacted, an amendment was passed allowing for a deduction for rent paid for dwellings.[6]

On April 14, 1864, a third bill was introduced. This one changed the rate to 5 percent (from 3 percent) on incomes over $600. Rep. Augustus Frank, Republican of New York, set off the first debate on progressivity by offering an amendment to add a 7.5 percent bracket for incomes between $10,000 and $25,000 and a 10 percent bracket for incomes over $25,000. "I offer the amendment," Frank said, "because I think it is just, right, and proper that those having a larger amount of income shall pay a larger amount of tax." (Frank was most sloppy: as we saw in chapter 2, the rich pay a larger amount under a flat rate and could even pay a larger amount with a regressive rate structure. Ten percent of $100,000 is more than 25 percent of $10,000.) But the Ways and Means Committee report said the "principle [of progressivity] was a vicious one." Stevens said he could "see no reason why a man should be punished in this way because he is rich." Sen. Justin Morrill of Vermont said unequal taxation amounted to confiscation.[7]

Frank's amendment was nevertheless adopted by the Ways and Means Committee. The Senate Finance Committee struck the 10 percent bracket. The full Senate applied the 7.5 percent rate to income over $5,000 (instead of $10,000). Another motion set a 10 percent rate for incomes over $15,000.

The conference committee lowered the threshold for the 10 percent rate from $15,000 to $10,000 and raised the rate on dividends and interest from 3 percent to 5 percent. Holders of government securities no longer paid a lower rate. The rental deduction was extended to owners.[8]

For the first time, tax returns had to be sworn, and government assessors could challenge returns. The penalty for late filing was doubled to 10 percent.

In addition, the Congress passed a special 5 percent tax on incomes over $600 for 1863 to pay for an army incentive program under which anyone who provided an acceptable recruit would be paid $2 and any person enlisting for three years would get the first month's pay in advance.[9]

The income tax by now was raising money. From a slow start of $2.7 million in 1862–63, it brought in $20.2 million the next year. The taste of that much money was apparently sweet to those who collected it. Treasury Secretary William P. Fessenden called for repeal of the exemption so that the tax would begin with dollar one. When he was a senator he expressed no opinion about progressivity. But as head of the Treasury he defended progressivity on the grounds that "the ability to pay increases in much more than arithmetical proportion as the amount of income exceeds the limit of reasonable necessity." The historian Harry Edwin Smith observed, "Many other men in public life seem to have gone through a similar experience in their attitude toward progressive rates."[10]

But before the latest act could take effect, a fourth bill was passed. Out of a belief that too many large-income earners were escaping the tax, Congress applied the 10 percent rate to incomes over $5,000. Government assessors were given the authority to increase the estimates of people's income. Penalties were increased: there was a 25 percent fine for neglecting or refusing to file. And the tax was to be doubled for a fraudulent return.[11]

None of the income-tax legislation prohibited making people's returns public, and when newspapers began asking for the returns the government agreed in order that "the amplest opportunity may be given for the detection of any fraudulent returns that may have been made." This naturally created antagonism toward the tax among those whose returns were of the greatest interest. In 1870 public release was outlawed.[12]

It should be noted that the government of the Confederacy

also passed a progressive income tax. It also passed a tax in kind, which authorized government officials to seize the fruits of production directly.[13]

Postbellum America

When the Civil War ended, the income tax continued in order to pay the interest on the Union's debt and to establish a sinking fund for the principal. But the attack on progressivity picked up again. Morrill argued that progressivity "can only be defended on the same ground that the highwayman defends his acts."[14] His opponents insisted that progressivity remain a feature of the tax until the regressive consumption taxes were removed. Some even called for increasing the top rate to 25 percent. There was also talk about raising the exemption because of the Civil War inflation.

In 1867 America's experiment with a progressive income tax ended. A tax bill was passed that eliminated the progressive rate structure and raised the exemption: a uniform rate of 5 percent would now be applied to all incomes over $1,000. The lessening demand for revenue seems to explain the loss of support for progressivity. The penalty for refusal to file was raised to 50 percent, but the penalty for failing to pay the tax when due dropped from 10 percent to 5 percent. The date for payment was moved from June 30 to April 30.[15]

In 1868 no more than 250,000 out of a population of 39.5 million paid the tax. This was down from nearly half a million in 1866.[16]

As the April 30, 1870, expiration date neared, there began a move to retain the income tax, led by the revenue department. Special Commissioner David Wells called for lowering the rate to 3 percent, arguing that revenues would hardly drop because people would be more truthful about their incomes.[17]

Three arguments, from various perspectives, were made against the tax at this time. First, Populists said that the tax was unjust because it did not distinguish between "earned" and "unearned" income. Second, outright income-tax opponents said it fostered fraud and evasion because the rates were so high. Third, those opponents also said it was inquisitorial, because government officials inquired into the affairs of citizens.[18] Defenders of the tax responded that the government needed the money and that the opposition came from rich, elite city dwellers.[19]

Congress approved a 2.5 percent rate and a $2,000 exemption. The tax expired in 1872 and for the first time since the Civil War, the United States had no income tax. By this time the federal government was running a surplus and many believed the tax was superfluous.

America's first experiment with income taxation was instructive. The tax quickly became an important revenue raiser. At its height in 1866 it raised 30 percent of internal revenues — $73 million — and nearly 19 percent of the net ordinary receipts of the federal government.[20]

Nearly two-thirds of that money was raised in three states. About one-third of the tax came from New York, with almost another one-third coming from Massachusetts and Pennsylvania. The area's heavy concentration of population and economic activity made this inevitable, and it was not missed by the people in the South and Midwest. It would become a big issue over the following twenty years.

The United States experienced great economic growth after the Civil War. Along with the boom came a great increase in duty-paying imports. That brought large surpluses to the U.S. Treasury for thirty years. The federal government kept the surplus down by paying pensions to Union veterans of the Civil War and their relatives. The pension program was arguably the first American welfare-state venture.

Although the surpluses hurt the case of those wishing to reinstate the income tax, sixty-eight bills were nevertheless introduced in Congress between 1874 and 1894. The tax was endorsed by the Greenback Party, the Farmers' Alliances, and the Populists, who saw it as a way to reduce the regressive tariff. Since the income tax would be paid by the rich and could relieve the poor from the tariff, it had the makings of an excellent political issue. The great fortunes being amassed by a small number of industrialists and businessmen made the issue ripe.

The Income Tax of 1894

As Grover Cleveland was resuming the presidency in 1893, a depression following a stock and bank panic hit the country and lasted until 1896. Unemployment reached 18 percent in 1894, with the figure for nonagricultural workers as high as 30 percent.[21] The budget surplus shrank.[22] The hardship created social unrest and protest. The economic upheaval worried the Democrats, for they feared they would lose ground to the Populists in the West and South. They also saw an opportunity to attack what they hated: the McKinley Tariff passed by the Republicans in 1890.

The result of these twin considerations was an income-tax

amendment. The South and Midwest led the effort for the tax, with the main opposition coming from the East.[23] The vote in the House was: 196 Democrats and 8 Populists for the bill; 122 Republicans, 17 Democrats, and 1 Populist against. In the Senate, only 2 votes from the Northeast were cast for the bill.[24] President Cleveland objected, but allowed it to become law without his signature.

The 1894 bill established a 2 percent flat tax on incomes from all sources, including wages and salaries, above $4,000 (about $50,000 today). It exempted interest on federal bonds issued with a prior exemption from taxes and the salaries of state and local officials, federal judges, and the president. Again, the tax hit very few people.

The argument for the tax once more centered on the belief that large incomes were untouched by the tax gatherers. Opponents predicted economic ruin and condemned the tax as "inquisitorial." Democrat Sen. David Hill of New York said, "It may be impracticable that our distinctively American experiment of individual freedom should go on."[25]

The Supreme Court Speaks

The U.S. Supreme Court would have the last word in the matter after hearing the case of *Pollock v. Farmers Loan and Trust Co.* in 1895. It took two hearings before the matter was resolved. In the first instance, the Court ruled that the bill's tax on rents and real estate was a direct tax and hence was invalid because, contrary to the U.S. Constitution, it was not levied proportionally on the states. The tax as applied to state and municipal bonds was also struck down. But the Court divided 4–4 (one justice was out sick) on the question of whether the tax on general income was unconstitutional.[26]

Because of the importance of the issue, the Court agreed to rehear the case when it was back to full strength. In a 5–4 vote, the Court stuck to its ruling on real estate and broadened it to include personal property. The fatal provisions sank the whole scheme. (The *Pollock* case reversed the 1881 Springer case, which upheld the Civil War tax and ruled that an income tax is not a direct tax.)

At this point something must be said about the distinction between direct and indirect taxes. The Constitution, in Article I, Sections 8 and 9, apparently draws the distinction by declaring that direct taxes, such as a "capitation" (or head or poll) tax, must be apportioned among the states according to the census. On the other hand, "Duties, Imposts and Excises shall be *uniform* throughout the United States." (Emphasis added.) This created a problem for advocates of income taxation: if the tax was direct, it had to be apportioned among the states; if it was indirect, the rate had to be uniform, or flat. The Sixteenth Amendment was intended to relieve the Congress of that dilemma.

In fact, the distinction between direct and indirect taxes was anything but clear. Many definitions have been offered over the years. For example, it has been suggested that a direct tax is one which the federal government levies on citizens straightaway; whereas an indirect tax is one levied on the states, which in turn tax their citizens. That was how revenue was raised under the Articles of Confederation. It has also been said that a direct tax is one that cannot be passed along to others, unlike a sales tax. That would make the income tax a direct tax.

At different times, the Supreme Court has held the income tax to be either a direct or an indirect tax. No less an authority on the Constitution than Alexander Hamilton said, "It is a matter of regret that terms so uncertain and vague in so important a point are to be found in the Constitution."[27] The confusion is further illustrated by the fact that when Rufus King of Massachusetts asked the Constitutional Convention what "direct taxation" meant, James Madison recorded in his notes, "No one answered."[28]

While the Supreme Court decided the case mostly on technical issues, Justice Stephen J. Field allowed himself a comment on more basic principles. He wrote that if a discriminatory tax is permitted to stand, "it will mark the hour when the sure decadence of our government will commence."[29] Justice John Harlan, leading the dissenters, wrote that the majority decision denied the national government a vital general power on which the very existence of the nation might someday depend.[30]

Opponents of the income tax won the day thanks to a sympathetic Supreme Court. It was to be a short-lived victory.

The Sixteenth Amendment

From 1895 to 1909 the income tax lost the spotlight, except for a vain attempt by Populists to use it to finance the Spanish-American war.[31] Nonetheless, the Democrats endorsed it in their 1896 platform and called for a constitutional amendment to nullify *Pollock* in their 1908 platform.[32] In 1908 former Republican president Theodore Roosevelt endorsed both an income tax and an inheritance tax.[33] He had much to say about a graduated income tax in 1904 when he was elected president, scorning what he called "swollen inheritances and incomes."[34] In their 1904 race against Roosevelt, the Democrats (with candidate New York State Judge Alton B. Parker) left the income tax out of their platform. But things changed over the next four years.

The beginning of the new century saw a big increase in the cost of living — one-third between 1897 and 1913.[35] The 1908 election brought a new group of liberal Republicans, called the Insurgents, to Congress. They joined with the Progressives to form an eight- to ten-member bloc of senators, mostly from the Midwest, that attacked the tariff and introduced income-tax legislation. A compromise worked out between nineteen Republican senators and the Democrats led to an income-tax amendment to a pending tariff bill. Republican Senate leader Nelson Aldrich of New York feared that the amendment would pass, so he delayed the vote for two months. Meanwhile, he asked President William Howard Taft to intervene. Taft offered a fateful compromise: immediate passage of a 4 percent excise tax on corporate profits and a constitutional amendment to allow an income tax without apportionment among the states.[36] This caused an odd reversal. The old-line Republicans, who opposed the income tax, supported the corporate tax, while the Insurgents opposed it as a poor substitute for an income tax. The compromise bill passed.

Taft, a Republican Progressive and a member of the influential pro-intervention National Civic Federation, had seemed to accept the income tax during his campaign, but was not convinced of the need for a constitutional amendment. He changed his mind in 1909. Noting that ratification may be difficult, he said he had "become convinced that a great majority of the people of this country are in favor of vesting the National Government with power to levy an income tax."[37]

In 1909, the income tax amendment passed overwhelmingly in both chambers of Congress. Rep. Sereno E. Payne, cosponsor of the then-pending Payne-Aldrich Tariff, was particularly concerned that, should the nation enter a war, "we have the power to exhaust every resource of taxing our people."[38]

The issues thrashed out during ratification were related to class and geography. The West and South eyed the greater Northeastern wealth, which they felt was untouched by federal taxation, and pushed the ability-to-pay principle. The public in these regions was told that most people would never pay the tax. Northeasterners complained that the tax would victimize them. Idaho Republican Sen. William Borah, trying to allay fears that the tax would become an "assault on wealth," said, "No sane man would take from industry its just reward or rob frugality of a fair and honest return."[39]

An issue that caused some concern in New York was the prospective taxation of state and municipal bonds. The Republican Gov. Charles Evans Hughes, who otherwise supported the amendment, was the leading opponent of taxing the bonds. Sen. Elihu Root, a conservative progressive and J. P. Morgan associate, defended the provision. Significantly, Taft urged Republican party leaders in New York to support the amendment, putting to rest the theory that he regarded the amendment process as the burial ground of the income tax.[40]

Hughes's concern was widely shared in New York, and the amendment went down to defeat in the legislature. The defeat was soon reversed, however. In 1910 the Democrats captured the statehouse and the governor's mansion. The amendment was ratified in a new vote. After a slow start, old-line Republican losses to Democrats and Republican Insurgents were enough to gain the needed thirty-six states. The last state ratified on February 13, 1913. States refusing to ratify or failing to act were Connecticut, Rhode Island, Pennsylvania, Virginia, Florida, and Utah. Those were the only states that did not undergo the political upheavals of 1910 and 1912 in which Republican Insurgents and Populist Democrats threw out the Republican organization or forced concessions on it. As the *Springfield Republican* put it, "The Sixteenth Amendment owes its existence mainly to the West and South, where individual incomes of $5,000 or over are comparatively few."[41]

Envy of the great new fortunes in the northeast fueled the drive for the income-tax amendment. But another conviction must also have been at work, at least for some supporters, namely, that the federal government ought to have access to greater revenues. Edwin L. Godkin, the libertarian editor of *The Nation*, warned, "With such a source of revenue put at its mercy, Congress will be more extravagant than ever"[42] He and others worried about the dangers of the government's new power. Virginia House Speaker Richard E. Byrd predicted that "a hand from Washington will be stretched out and placed upon every man's business.... Heavy fines imposed by distant and unfamiliar tribunals will constantly menace the tax payer. An army of Federal officials, spies and detectives will descend upon the state.... "[43]

On the other side, *The New York Evening Post* wrote that the income tax would permit the lowering of the tariff to the benefit of consumers. Many free traders naively hoped that would be the case. But the income tax never brought about a cut in the tariff. Quite the contrary; in 1930 tariffs hit historic highs. Nor should anyone have expected otherwise, for now that the tariff was no longer needed to raise revenue, it was fully available for protective purposes. That was something that seems not to have occurred to free traders, with the exception of the libertarian sociologist William Graham Sumner. An effective revenue tariff by definition is a weak protective tariff; conversely, a strong protective tariff is a weak revenue tariff. If the tariff is to raise lots of money, it cannot be high enough to keep consumers from buying imports; if it prices imports out of reach, it will not raise much money.[44] Before the income tax, the lawmakers had to find a happy medium between revenue and protection. With the income tax, it was freed from that restriction.

America Gets an Income Tax

Woodrow Wilson was elected president in 1912 against two Progressive opponents, former president Theodore Roosevelt, running on the Bull Moose ticket, and the incumbent Republican, Taft. Wilson's platform called for an income tax, and in April 1913, he called a special session of Congress. A graduated income tax was added to the Underwood Tariff and passed.

The United States now had an income tax. A few years after the tax was enacted, the Supreme Court gave its blessing to progressivity with little comment.[45]

While politicians put the income tax through, we must not underrate the role played by the Progressive intellectuals. As advocates of government activism, they wanted the state to be able to raise huge sums of money. The income tax filled the bill. In their campaign to win acceptance for the tax, these intellectuals took two tacks. First, they argued that it was necessary for the modern state to fulfill its new and expanded role. Second, as we saw in chapter 2, intellectuals such as Edwin R. A. Seligman argued that social evolution had selected "ability to pay" as a just principle of taxation.

It is generally assumed that wealthy businessmen unanimously opposed the income tax from the beginning. But the story is more complicated. In his book *Businessmen and Reform*, Robert Wiebe writes, "When they faced a graduated income tax in 1913, businessmen everywhere judged it the most destructive legislation in the nation's history."[46] This judgment may have been hasty. Carolyn Webber and Aaron Wildavsky said that "businessmen who preferred predictability" joined the pro-income tax side.[47]

Many businessmen, particularly the owners of the biggest businesses, clearly created an environment for the income tax by their support for such government activism as the tariff, the Interstate Commerce Commission, and other agencies.[48] Their opposition to laissez faire undercut any opposition they might have raised against other government intervention.

There are indications that some businessmen welcomed the income tax because without it the government would be barred from certain undertakings that would benefit them. As the nineteenth century entered its last decade and America embarked on an imperialist policy in Asia, some businessmen became newly interested in world trade. This was not the nineteenth-century, pacificistic, free-trade philosophy of Cobden and Bright but rather a military-commercial policy that called on the U.S. government — and its armed might if necessary — to "open" to American business foreign markets dominated by rival colonial powers. The Open Door policy for China is an example. This is also the period when there was a major push for a big navy, led by Adm. Alfred Mahan and the Navy League. The growth in American exports helped broaden the constituency for the income tax.[49]

The 1913 income tax rate was put at 1 percent on net income after a personal exemption of $3,000, some credits, and an additional $1,000 exemption for married couples living together. There was also a graduated 2 percent to 7 percent surcharge on incomes from $20,000 to $500,000. Interest on state and municipal bonds was exempt.[50]

In 1913, the average personal income was $621. Only 2 percent of the population was liable for the tax between 1913 and 1915.[51] Eighty percent of the returns were filed by people involved in business; 17 percent were in the professions, 3.3 percent in agriculture, 0.5 percent were laborers. Businessmen reported 85 percent of the income and paid almost 90 percent of the revenues.[52]

Given the level of incomes in those days, it was a tax aimed strictly at the richest people in the country. If the system were in place today, a single person making less than about $45,000 (the bottom 75 percent of filers) would pay no tax. A couple earning less than $60,000 would pay nothing. Incomes up to $300,000 would be in the 1 percent bracket. Someone would have to make $7.5 million before paying the top 7 percent rate. In 1994 dollars, the exemptions of 1913 would be worth $44,776 for single people and $59,701 for married couples.[53]

Returns from the tax at first were disappointing to tax collectors: $28 million in 1914. They picked up thereafter: $41 million in 1915 and nearly $68 million in 1916.[54] The tax accounted for only 10 percent of revenues until 1915.[55] As usual, it was war that gave the boost to government power. More than $1 billion was raised during World War I, making the income tax the permanent major part of the revenue system.[56]

The Rates Go Up

The rates followed a similar path. From 1913 to 1915, the top rate was 7 percent. In 1916, it was 15 percent. Then: 67 percent in 1917 and 77 percent in 1918, the war years. An excess-profits tax was added in those years. The personal exemption, which in 1915 was $3,000 for a single person and $4,000 for married couples with two dependents, fell, respectively, to $1,000 and $2,400 in 1917. Despite this, it still was not a tax on most of the population. But the war shifted the federal government away from consumption taxes, such as the tariff, to income, profits, and estate taxes.[57]

After the war, the top rate fell only to 73 percent because of the debt. It declined in the 1920s to a low of 24 percent in 1929. Note that it got nowhere near the prewar 7 percent. With the Great Depression the rate headed back up under President Herbert Hoover and a Republican Congress: 25 percent in 1930, then 63 percent in 1932. In the New Deal, the top rate continued upward: 79 percent in 1936, 81 percent in 1940. It hit its high of 94 percent in 1944–45. From there it stayed in the 90s and 80s until 1964, when it dropped to 77 percent. In 1982 it was reduced to 50 percent. The Reagan tax reform of the late 1980s brought the top rate down to 28 percent.[58] That was the end of the decline. In 1990 President Bush, in violation of a campaign pledge not to raise taxes, hiked the rate to 31 percent. Then President Clinton in 1993 raised it to 39.6 percent.

The lowest rate moved up in fits and starts. Until 1915 the rate was 1 percent up to $20,000. In 1917, it was 2 percent up to $2,000, then 6 percent up to $4,000. By 1941 the bottom rate was at 10 percent up to $2,000. It hit its high of 23 percent in 1945. Today it stands at 15 percent on income up to $29,750.[59]

It took World War II to make the income tax a truly universal tax. In 1940, fewer than fifteen million tax returns were filed. In 1950 the number was more than fifty-three million. The war initiated millions of Americans into the world of the income tax.[60] In 1939 the income tax raised $1 billion. In 1945 it raised $19 billion.[61] The most lucrative revenue pool was not the wealthy — there

81

weren't enough of them. Middle-class and working-class taxpayers represented the biggest potential for revenue.

The U.S. Treasury began withholding taxes from paychecks in 1943. It was a measure designed to avoid financing the war by inflation, according to Milton Friedman, who worked on the Treasury group that devised the system.[62] When the war ended, withholding continued. It has been a key method of making the income tax seem less onerous than it really is.

The 1970s demonstrated that hiking rates is not necessary to raise additional revenue. Inflation pushed taxpayers into higher tax brackets, although their incomes were no higher in real terms. The government raked in the money, until interventionist policies produced both inflation and recession, so-called stagflation. "Bracket-creep" ended in the 1980s when the tax brackets were indexed to inflation. (However, the capital gains tax has not been indexed; people still pay taxes on illusory gains.)

Lessons to Be Learned

The history of the income tax produced at least three lessons that should not be ignored. First, a tax that was supposed to hit only the rich eventually became one that has harmed the middle and working classes. In the aggregate, the biggest bucks for the government will always be in those classes. There are not enough superrich to support the government for long. Envy can boomerang.

The second lesson is that if the government is given access to a huge pool of revenue, it will take full advantage of it. Adjusted for inflation, government spending, from enactment of the income tax in 1913 to 1994, increased 13,592 percent. The portion of federal revenue from personal and corporate taxes jumped from 7 percent in 1913 to over 54 percent in 1994. As a percentage of gross domestic product, those taxes went from 0.1 percent to 10 percent.[63] The income tax has given the federal government a staggering leverage over the economic life of America.

The third lesson comes from the fact that some people were attracted to the income tax by the promise that it would permit reduction of the tariff, which imposed a hardship on people of modest means. But it did not work out that way. America got the income tax and kept the tariff. That should teach us something about government and the danger of striving to replace one tax with another rather than pushing for simple repeal. As Frank Chodorov observed, "It promised to make the swap, and perhaps its leaders believed the promise, but the nature of government is such that it cannot give up one power for another; not permanently, at any rate."[64]

The income tax has been a disaster for the American people. In the chapter that follows, we will examine how we could get along without it.

Notes

¹ John F. Witte, *The Politics and Development of the Federal Income Tax* (Madison, Wis.: University of Wisconsin Press, 1985), p. 67.

² Jeffrey Rogers Hummel, *Emancipating Slaves, Enslaving Free Men: A History of the American Civil War* (Chicago: Open Court, 1996), p. 222.

³ Witte, p. 67.

⁴ Ibid., p. 53.

⁵ Ibid., p. 69.

⁶ Harry Edwin Smith, *The United States Federal Internal Tax History from 1861 to 1871* (Boston: Houghton Mifflin Co., 1941), pp. 54, 56; Hummel, p. 223.

⁷ Smith, p. 59.

⁸ Ibid., pp. 61–62.

⁹ Ibid., p. 64.

¹⁰ Both quotations are at ibid., p. 65.

¹¹ Ibid., p. 66.

¹² Ibid., pp. 67–68.

¹³ Hummel, p. 227.

¹⁴ Quoted in Smith, p. 70.

¹⁵ Ibid., pp. 74–75.

¹⁶ Ibid., p. 77.

¹⁷ Ibid., p. 78.

¹⁸ Ibid., p. 79.

¹⁹ Ibid., p. 80.

²⁰ Ibid., p. 93, and Bennett D. Baack and Edward John Ray, "Special Interests and the Adoption of the Income Tax in the United States," *Journal of Economic History* 45 (September 1985): 608.

²¹ Robert Higgs, *Crisis and Leviathan: Episodes in the Growth of the American Government* (New York: Oxford University Press, 1987), p. 84.

²² Edward Stanwood, *American Tariff Controversies in the Nineteenth Century*, vol. 1 (Boston: Houghton Mifflin, 1903), p. 296.

²³ Witte, p. 71.

²⁴ Baack and Ray, pp. 609–10.

²⁵ Arthur A. Ekirch Jr., "The Sixteenth Amendment: The His-

torical Background," *Cato Journal* 1 (Spring 1981): 168.

[26] Ibid., pp. 168–69.

[27] Quoted in John D. Buenker, *The Income Tax and the Progressive Era* (New York: Garland, 1985), p. 17.

[28] Charles Adams, *For Good and Evil: The Impact of Taxes on the Course of Civilization* (Lanham, Md.: Madison Books, 1993), p. 313.

[29] Quoted in Adams, p. 370.

[30] Richard Hofstadter, ed., *Great Issues in American History*, vol. 2, 1864–1957 (New York: Vintage, 1959), pp. 120–21.

[31] Witte, p. 74.

[32] Ekirch, pp. 171–72.

[33] "Roosevelt was the first President of the United States who openly proposed to use the powers of political government for the purpose of affecting the distribution of wealth in the interest of the golden mean." Charles A. Beard and Mary R. Beard, *The Rise of American Civilization* (New York: Macmillan, 1936), p. 596.

[34] Ibid.

[35] John D. Buenker, "The Ratification of the Federal Income Tax Amendment," *Cato Journal* 1 (Spring 1981): 186.

[36] Witte, p. 75.

[37] Ekirch, p. 173.

[38] Ibid., p. 174.

[39] Ibid., p. 176.

[40] Buenker, "Ratification of the Federal Income Tax Amendment," p. 215.

[41] Ekirch, p. 178.

[42] Ibid., p. 177.

[43] Ibid., pp. 177–78.

[44] Frank Chodorov, *The Income Tax: Root of All Evil* (New York: Devin-Adair, 1954), pp. 40–41. The tariff in that respect is like any "sin" tax, such as the tax on tobacco. If it really discourages smoking, it doesn't raise much money. Come to think of it, a tariff is a sin tax, a tax on the "sin" of buying imports. See William F. Shughart II, ed., *Taxing Choice: The Predatory Politics of Fiscal Discrimination* (New Brunswick, N.J.: Transaction Publishers, 1996).

[45] Adams, p. 368.

[46] Robert H. Wiebe, *Businessmen and Reform: A Study of the Progressive Movement* (Chicago: Quadrangle Paperbacks, 1968), p. 196.

[47] Carolyn Webber and Aaron Wildavsky, *A History of Taxation and Expenditure in the Western World* (New York: Simon and Schuster, 1986), p. 421.

[48] Gabriel Kolko, *The Triumph of Conservatism: A Reinterpretation of American History, 1900–1916* (Chicago: Quadrangle Books, 1967) and *Railroads and Regulation, 1887–1916* (Princeton, N.J.: Princeton University Press, 1965).

[49] Bennett D. Baack and Edward John Ray, "The Political Economy of the Origin and Development of the Federal Income Tax" in *Emergence of Modern Political Economy*, ed. Robert Higgs (Greenwich, Conn.: JAI Press, 1985), pp. 127–31.

[50] Ekirch, p. 180.

[51] Webber and Wildavsky, p. 421.

[52] Buenker, "Ratification of the Federal Income Tax Amendment," p. 188.

[53] Raymond J. Keating, "Original Intent and the Income Tax," *The Freeman*, February 1996, p. 71.

[54] Ekirch, pp. 181–82.

[55] Webber and Wildavsky, p. 422.

[56] Ekirch, p. 182.

[57] Higgs, pp. 151–52.

[58] Joseph A. Pechman, *Federal Tax Policy*, 5th ed. (Washington, D.C.: Brookings Institution, 1987), p. 313.

[59] Ibid.

[60] Higgs, p. 231.

[61] John C. Chrommie, *The Internal Revenue Service* (New York: Praeger Publishers, 1970), pp. 21–22.

[62] "Best of Both Worlds" (an interview with Milton Friedman), *Reason*, June 1995, p. 33. Friedman recalls that the IRS opposed withholding because it was a departure from its standard method of collecting revenue.

[63] Keating, p. 71.

[64] Chodorov, p. 40.

6

Let's Abolish the Income Tax

C an we live without the Sixteenth Amendment, the income tax, and the Internal Revenue Service?

After all that has been said in the preceding chapters, it might be better to ask if we can continue to live with them. We have seen that the income tax is based on a fundamentally immoral notion: that the state has a prior claim on the fruits of a person's labor. That notion, which is a half-step removed from the slave principle, is at odds with the Jeffersonian idea that lies at the foundation of the American Republic: that every human being has a natural right to life, liberty, and the pursuit of happiness, which of necessity includes the right to use and dispose of honestly acquired property.

We have seen further that when the state is permitted to tax income a process is set in motion that inevitably reverses the traditional American relationship between citizen and government. In the original Jeffersonian vision the citizen was the master and the government was the servant. But with the advent of income taxation, that relationship began to change and eventually was reversed. When government seeks to tax income it will inevitably assume the powers required to carry out that mission. Those powers will enable it to delve deeply into people's personal affairs, destroying their financial privacy, putting them permanently on the defensive, and leaving them vulnerable to demands that they prove they have not violated the law. Intentions are irrelevant. Admit the principle of income taxation and all those things follow logically. Citizens become subjects.

We have also seen that income taxation undermines the market economy. By draining the people's savings and capital, the tax necessarily impedes their ability to create prosperity, to achieve financial independence, and to make a better society for everyone. Meanwhile, the income tax gives the state unprecedented access to wealth, bringing in huge revenues with which politicians and bureaucrats can attempt to shape society according to their liking and buy political support so they may stay in power and tax some more. We have seen how the policymakers use the tax code to encourage and discourage behavior arbitrarily, undermining the spontaneous productive forces of society. Adam Smith's invisible hand has been turned into the very visible pointing finger and clenched fist of the politicians and tax authorities.

Income taxation has made the modern American megastate what it is. In *The Rights of Man*, Thomas Paine wrote that government does not raise taxes so it can fight wars; rather, it fights wars so it can raise taxes. Whichever is the case, the power to tax incomes has freed the national government to venture full-force into areas foreign and domestic in which it had, at worst, only dabbled in the days before the Sixteenth Amendment.

Since World War II, the personal income tax has been the largest source of federal revenue. In fiscal year 1997, it was expected to raise more than $791 billion, more than 45 percent of all receipts, in a budget of more than $1.7 trillion. (That share has dropped slightly in recent years.) The corporation income tax was expected to bring in almost $198 billion more (12 percent), and the category known as "social insurance taxes and retirement receipts" — payroll taxes — was to capture more than $596 billion more (34 percent). That is more than $1.5 trillion from individual and business income. The people's income has proven to be a mother lode for the U.S. government. Cut off from that kind of money, the size and scope of government would shrink fast. Imagine what would be possible with that amount left in people's pockets!

Of course, a $1.5 trillion tax cut — not to be replaced with new taxes — would leave "only" about $200 billion for the government to spend. Admittedly, that is a radical reduction in the size of government. (For some, however, it may be too small a cut.) How would it manage? Maybe it is not as drastic as it looks. A government that lived up to the Jeffersonian vision would not have to spend a lot of money. If it were reduced to the core functions spelled out in the Constitution (essentially territorial defense and courts to handle the few crimes put under federal jurisdiction), perhaps $200 billion would be too much money.

According to the Office of Management and Budget, the federal government in 1941 spent, in 1987 dollars, about $135 billion. A year later, it spent $315 billion. That government was hardly Jeffersonian in scope, considering that the New Deal was in place and the United States was increasing military spending in anticipation of involvement in the new European war. From 1947 to 1951, the government spent between $193 billion and $286 billion a year (1987 dollars). The budget was in surplus four of those five years. Again, that government was not small. The New Deal had not been rolled back, and the Cold War was beginning. If that government could get by on less than $300 billion, why can't today's government? True, income taxes raised the major part of even those budgets. But alternative, voluntary financing would have an easier time raising $300 billion than $1.3 trillion. There is nothing magic about $300 billion. It just happens to be what's left if all income taxation were abolished.

The Burden of Government Spending

Too many discussions about changes in the tax system try to avoid the issue of government spending. They tend to accept "revenue neutrality" as an opening condition. Reforms are designed so that the tax system will raise the same amount of revenue as the current system (if not more). Revenue neutrality aims at separating two issues: the structure of the tax system and the amount of revenue raised. It is a device to simplify discussion. Tax reformers wish to propose changes in the tax structure without saying how they would cut the federal budget to adjust for lower revenues. Any suggested spending cut, of course, would prompt opposition to the whole plan from whoever benefitted from that spending. Critics of lower taxes have shrewdly used the public's concern about the federal deficit to attack any tax plan that can be shown to "lose" revenue. Revenue neutrality is a concession to those critics.

The supply-siders avoid the revenue-neutrality ground rule through the Laffer effect. The economist Arthur Laffer popularized the idea that government can increase revenues by lowering tax rates. The rates can be so high that people shelter, hide, and even abstain from earning income. Reduced rates can make such tax avoidance unnecessary. So rate cuts can increase revenues and have done so before.

While the Laffer effect is sound, raising revenue is not a good reason to cut tax rates — which brings up the alternative to the revenue-neutral and revenue-enhancing rules. It is the revenue-cutting rule: reducing government revenues is a good thing. The wisdom of that rule is rooted in the fact that people have a right to their money and know better how to spend it than government does. Moreover, when government spends people's money, it mostly does mischief. The rule suggests another approach to tax reform, one that combines a discussion of the tax structure with the amount of revenue. The weight of government includes total spending (revenues raised plus borrowing) as well as the method of tax collection. (The burden of regulation is put aside for this discussion.) The burden of the income tax is directly related to how much it raises. To address how taxes are collected without looking at the amount raised, or vice versa, is to cheat the taxpayers.

No New Taxes

Thus the proper response to an indictment of the income tax is not a new tax designed to raise the same amount of money. Any alternative tax that can raise what income taxes today raise would be, for that reason alone, a burdensome tax. True, a different tax might be less intrusive of civil liberties. Then again, it might not be. A sufficiently high tax of any nature will stimulate evasion, which in turn could prompt the government to take draconian measures. Empirically, if not theoretically, the income tax is an especially bad tax. But any tax intended to raise more than a trillion dollars a year is, by definition, confiscatory, even in a $7 trillion economy. If an alternative tax is less intrusive than the income tax, that simply means the government can engage in a less painful form of confiscation. But that could allow even greater levels of confiscation precisely because the tax inflicts less "collateral" pain.

The only way to avoid taxes that raise $1 trillion is for the federal government to spend far less than it spends today. Real slashes in spending cannot be made by half-hearted attempts to eliminate "waste, fraud, and abuse." Only completely rethinking the idea of government can accomplish that.

What Goverment Should *Not* Do

Thus, a book on the income tax appropriately ends with a discussion of what government should *not* be doing. Once people are clear on that issue they will be less likely to acquiesce in a tax system that extracts astronomical revenues. Few people want any tax for its own sake. If they support, or abstain from opposing, a tax, it is usually because they want whatever the revenue can finance. (There are exceptions: the especially envious might simply want to see high-income people dispossessed, and puritans, driven by, in H. L. Mencken's words, the "haunting fear that somewhere someone is happy," support "sin taxes" to discourage drinking and smoking.) Thus, if people give up their attachment to expansive government, they will feel free to fight the income tax.

In the original Jeffersonian, or libertarian, vision of America, the federal government had a few specified constitutional functions. Under the U.S. Constitution the federal government was permitted to exercise no powers other than those delegated by that document. All other powers were reserved to the states or the people. It is important to keep that framework in mind. If a power was not specified, the federal government could not assume it. That point was made over and over when, during the ratification debates, people demanded a Bill of Rights. Why is there a need for a Bill of Rights, defenders of the proposed Constitution asked? The federal government can do only the few things expressly delegated. Alexander Hamilton wondered why a prohibition on abridging the freedom of the press was necessary, when the Constitution granted the government no power to regulate the press in the first place.

As a result of that philosophy, the federal government was limited. It has been noted that for much of the nineteenth century, an American could live his life without having contact with a federal official, except a postmaster.

The Progressive Mindset

Somewhere along the line, the Founders' philosophy was turned on its head. Presidents, congressmen, judges, statist intellectuals, and later almost everyone else came to believe that the federal government should be able to do anything that is not expressly prohibited. That was the essence of the Progressive mindset. In the Progressive world-view, government needs the flexibility to respond to any contingency, to address any social problem, to right any wrong, to relieve any pain. Progressives did not like the antiquated thinking that saw the Constitution as a barrier to government expansion. The "living Constitution" was born. That benign-sounding phrase (coined later) was conjured up to justify changing the Constitution, without formal amendment, from a limit on power to a blank check. What was impermissible to the federal government by an earlier interpretation became permissible once the Constitution was construed as an evolving document. But by that philosophy, the Constitution is no limit on government power at all. A constitutional government that defines its own powers is a contradiction in terms.

The early advocates of big government in America were offended that entrepreneurs were amassing fortunes in the industrial revolution. They were offended by income disparities. They were offended by new-fangled factories. They were offended by the poverty that had always existed but which the new prosperity now made more conspicuous. They failed to realize that free-market capitalism did not create poverty and was steadily reducing it. They looked at the remains of the older, precapitalist world and assumed it was the fault of economic freedom and property rights. Thus, they wanted the Constitution to accommodate their aspirations to restrict, if not do away with, economic freedom and private property.

Many of the people prospering under capitalism also wanted a new role for the state. Finding the competitive, profit-and-loss system too uncertain, businessmen often turned to government for protection from foreign and domestic competitors. Taxes, subsidies, and regulations often were intended to help one group against others. Few people, it turned out, were willing to take their chances with freedom and free enterprise. They felt more comfortable with a little insurance from the government.

But for the government to play the role of economic and social insurer, it must get into the wealth-transfer racket. Increasingly, government took wealth from producers and gave it to nonproducers because it had no resources of its own. Although from the beginning the federal government engaged in some transfer activities (the tariff primarily), the Progressives helped turn it into a veritable transfer machine. The machine became a monster thanks to two world wars, the New Deal, and the Cold War. While taxation for the purpose of defense and internal improvements appeared to be for the general welfare (though that spending was rife with transfers also), more and more of what government did looked as though it was intended to help particular interests at the general population's expense in order to win political support.

Eventually it became accepted by almost everyone that the government was there to provide "services." Today there is no shame in seeking favors that others must pay for. Gone are the days when congressmen could vote against appropriations to relieve some hardship on grounds that the Constitution does not authorize charity. It is hard to know whether the people seeking government favors ever admit to themselves that the money first has to be taken from others before it can be given to them. Perhaps they rationalize by thinking that the money belongs to everyone. Or maybe they think that if they don't take the money someone else will. However they explain it, the moral compunction against asking the state to steal from one's neighbor gradually weakened and disappeared. The unwritten moral constitution of the people, without which a written constitution is virtually worthless, has taken a dramatic turn from the days of the nation's founding.

A Right to the Loot

Today it is not unusual to hear retired people say they have a right to Social Security benefits even if they know they receive more than they paid while working. It is a rare business owner who objects on principle to protective tariffs or subsidies. How many middle-class parents object to government college loans for their children? Getting something apparently for nothing has become acceptable, even shrewd. Of course, it is not "for nothing," since, as Frederic Bastiat put it, everyone tries to live at everyone else's expense. People see the favors they get, but they don't compare them to what it costs to provide favors to others.

The irony is that even people who claim to support limits on government power play the transfer game. The late libertarian teacher Robert LeFevre used to ask conservative businessmen to list the government activities they liked. These people, who claimed to favor limited government, would each write a short list of programs. The lists would differ, though; so when they were consolidated, the result was a government that had its hands in many areas of the economy. The point of LeFevre's exercise was that the political process can produce big government even when self-styled limited-government advocates are calling the shots.

Observe the transfer state in action. Social Security imposes taxes on working people and hands the money to retired people. Medicare does almost the same thing, except the money goes to doctors and hospitals. Agricultural programs take money from taxpayers and consumers and give it to farmers for not growing or for growing particular crops. Welfare programs give the taxpayers' money to people who do not work. Subsidies reward well-connected business people with the hard-earned money of the middle-class and working class. Foreign aid indirectly subsidizes particular American businesses by giving tax money to foreign governments that will buy American products and services. Government cultural agencies transfer wealth to artists, musicians, broadcasters, and humanities scholars. The education bureaucracy subsidizes trendy social experiments on children. The defense bureaucracy floods contractors with cash for equipment that is not needed and for missions that are improper. The list goes on and on.

In each case, people seeking reelection and aspiring to prestigious "public" careers extract wealth from the general population to finance their schemes and benefit those with the time and resources to gain influence. The textbook model of democratic government responsive to the people is not found in the real world. Rather, government is a vast auction hall (to use Mencken's metaphor) in which people enter bids for access to politicians and the vast booty collected by the tax system.

Can that ever be reversed? It won't be easy. Several things stand in the way. As mentioned, the state has engaged in its transfer activities so long that most people don't think of it as expropriation any longer. The few bones thrown its way (such as student loans) keep the unorganized middle class from raising a fuss, although if people paid attention they would see that the system costs them more than they get back in subsidies. In case an average citizen decides to look more closely, the government has made it difficult to learn what it is really up to. It engages in deception and obfuscation to shroud the plunder. Try reading a typical piece of legislation some time. Chances are you will give up after a couple of paragraphs. It is not meant to be accessible to lay people. The same goes for the budgets written by the president and the Congress, and the regulations churned out by the regulatory mill. Whether by design or by accident, the process of government has become so esoteric that it encourages what economists call "rational ignorance." By making it expensive to become an informed citizen, the policymakers ensure that fewer people will find it worthwhile to learn what is really going on — and to perhaps rock the boat. Complexity breeds apathy. Apathy breeds incumbency. Thus the "ins" perpetuate their rule at the expense of nearly everyone else.

Thomas Jefferson understood that. It was he who said that the price of liberty is eternal vigilance and that the natural tendency is for government to grow and liberty to yield. The second statement implies a lack of confidence that the people can be counted on to exercise eternal vigilance. Liberty after a while is taken for granted. People understandably turn to such concerns as making a living and raising families. They leave the hen house to the foxes. It is a perverse form of the division of labor.

The Unwritten Constitution

The written Constitution was never enough to stop the growth of government. Constitutions are always interpreted by officers of the state, who usually have an interest in weakening any limits. The paper document must be buttressed by an unwritten constitution in the hearts and minds of the people. That is what provides the ultimate limits on the state. When that constitution is weak and deferential to power, the state grows. When it is jealous of liberty, as Jefferson hoped, government is held in check. The tragic story of America lies in the weakening of the people's unwritten constitution and the resultant growth of government power. Author Joseph Sobran illustrates this by noting that for many years presidents used their inaugural speeches to assure the public that they understood and would respect the limits on the federal government set by the Constitution. That's how deeply the people cared about those limits. But for decades we have heard little from presidents and other leaders about constitutional limits. It's now a quaint notion. Only once in the past sixty years has the U.S. Supreme Court ruled that Congress overstepped its constitutional bounds set by the Commerce Clause, for example.

Can the unwritten constitution be revived? If it is possible at all, it will be accomplished only through a libertarian moral revival. People will have to become excited about liberty once more. Fourth of July lip service to freedom will not be enough. What is needed is the orneriness about intrusions on their liberty that the colonists and first Americans exhibited. When the residents of the colonies got mad at the Crown's stamp and tea taxes, they were showing a sensitivity to taxes that has not been seen in the United States for a long time. A libertarian moral revival would include that kind of high sensitivity to any talk about higher or new taxes. It would also prompt opposition to welfare-state programs, economic regulation, violations of civil liberties, and intervention in foreign conflict, on grounds that those all diminish freedom. The revival would see the megastate as the major threat in the world today.

In sum, when people come to understand what liberty truly means, and when they value it as much as they say they do, they will be far less tolerant of government. They will be appalled at a political process that takes their money and gives it to their fellow citizens, with the politicians and bureaucrats taking a hefty cut in the process. They will be outraged at a tax system that treats them like milch cows.

People must again believe that liberty is a necessity, not a luxury. Why is liberty important? Political liberty is the absence of aggressive physical force (and fraud). It is the condition in which people control their persons and their legitimate possessions without physical interference by others. Liberty is important because people need it to live as human beings. The human way of life requires thinking, planning, and the production of values for consumption or exchange. If people are to be able fully to engage in those activities, they need an environment in which their rights to life, liberty, and property are respected. The threat to those rights from common criminals is an ever-present danger. But it cannot compare with the threat that government has posed to mankind, especially in the twentieth century.

There are some hopeful signs. A few years ago 39 percent of Americans polled by the Gallup organization said that the federal government was an "immediate threat" to their liberty. Fifty-two percent endorsed the sentiment when the word "immediate" was removed. Libertarian ideas are discussed more prominently in the news media than they have been in decades. Indeed, the word "libertarian" has entered the mainstream political lexicon.

A Libertarian Crusade

What will turn this modest start into a full-fledged libertarian crusade? No one can say for sure, but it will certainly require a multipronged effort. It will no doubt include economic analysis of how much wealth the government drains from people's pockets via taxation and regulation. But that won't be enough. It will also require a moral appeal declaring that violations of liberty do not merely take points off the gross domestic product but also make society less human and humane. The heroic men who launched the American Revolution understood the power of such an appeal. We see in their example how the moral case for freedom could bring about American independence from what was the world's most powerful empire. That was a phenomenal achievement and a tribute to the power of an idea. If a moral crusade for liberty could succeed once, it can succeed again.

The crusade has to start somewhere. What better opening target than the income tax? It combines the most egregious features of government power: theft, intimidation, violation of privacy, and arbitrariness. It is the perfect device for teaching people about the threat of power. According to the Tax Foundation, the biggest tax burden that the American people face is the tax on earnings. At the median income, a two-earner couple works eighty-seven days a year to pay their federal income and payroll taxes. Ironically, because of the structure of the income tax, that burden increases when the economy grows and falls when the economy slows. Americans are punished for being productive. (All taxes at all levels required the average American to work 128 days in 1996.) Besides the financial burden, Americans must also endure the threat of an inquisition by the tax authorities if they are singled out for investigation.

Abolition vs. Reform

A campaign against the Sixteenth Amendment, the income tax, and the Internal Revenue Service would be doubly valuable. It would move us toward the explicit goal of abolition, and it would prepare people for the campaigns to follow against other forms of tyranny. The income tax cannot be reformed, because taxation of income has no place in a free society. It calls into being a multitude of evils that should offend anyone who values liberty. It has parallels with the slavery that once blotted America. The parallels extend even to the proposals for opposition. Some opponents of slavery called for gradual emancipation because they thought immediate freedom for slaves would harm them and disrupt the economy of South. Some even suggested that slave owners be compensated for their "losses."

Similarly, some opponents of the income tax wish to modify the system by going to a flat rate and other forms of simplification, such as elimination of deductions. Whether such reform is intended as an end in itself or as a gradual step toward abolition of the income tax, the flat tax is a bad idea. Flat-tax advocates are willing to trade tax deductions for a lower single rate, ignoring that rates can be added and raised in the future. More important, the flat tax affirms the principle of income taxation and keeps the IRS in place. But it is the very principle of income taxation that permits most of the evils discussed in this book. We must cut the poisonous vine out at the root. Trimming the leaves is not enough.

In the debate over slavery, the abolitionists represented by William Lloyd Garrison declared that "gradualism in theory is perpetuity in practice." They knew that the political process could reverse reforms at any time. Small steps won't get us where we want to go either. They can be co-opted by the defenders of the status quo, and they give the people too little stake in a drawn-out reform process. Abolition of the income tax, on the other hand, is something people can rally around because the benefits are palpable. The shining vision of a future free of income taxation is something that can energize people for the long struggle.

Thus we should apply Garrison's principle to the fight against the income tax. We must call for nothing less — and settle for nothing less — than the end of the Sixteenth Amendment, all taxation of income, and the IRS. That is the indispensable step on the road to freedom.

Afterword

In the summer of 1998, amid great fanfare, Congress passed, and President Clinton signed, a taxpayer "bill of rights." Republicans and Democrats alike hailed the IRS "overhaul" as the dawn of a new day, when the agency would be transformed from inquisitor to service agency.

This is the third so-called "bill of rights" for taxpayers passed in a decade. That fact alone should make anyone skeptical that real taxpayer relief is to be expected.

At first glance, the bill might look as though it will afford some protection for taxpayers. It creates a nine-member board to oversee operations, six of whose members will be from the private sector. (Journalist Jim Bovard points out it will also include a representative of the IRS employees' union.) The bill would also shift the burden of proof from the taxpayer to the IRS in court cases. Currently, the taxpayer is guilty until he proves himself innocent. Other provisions would let citizens harmed by IRS negligence sue for damages and would relieve taxpayers of liabilities of former spouses. Homes could no longer be seized without a court order. Some penalties would be reduced and some IRS deadlines tightened.

But in the world of legislation, especially IRS "reform" legislation, things, as W. S. Gilbert wrote, "are seldom what they seem."

The oversight board and the shift in the burden of proof "are said to be the silver bullets that will end IRS abuse," writes Daniel J. Pilla, one of the great IRS watchers, in the *National Review*. "They are more likely to be blank cartridges."[1]

Pilla writes that the oversight board is not what we were led to believe it would be. To judge by the news summaries, you'd think that this board would be able to come to the rescue of battered citizens. But that's not the case. The new body will be involved in planning for the future and in overseeing the IRS budget and commissioner. "In other words," writes Pilla, "the Board will function as a forum for thinking about the overall direction of the IRS." It won't have the power to prevent agents from treating taxpayers like child molesters. Pilla notes that the board is specifically denied authority over the agency's law-enforcement apparatus. Don't expect it to rectify the abuses associated with audits, seizures, and other activities designed to wring more revenue out of Americans. The board will not be able to avert the tyrannical conduct citizens reported in horrifying detail at Senate Finance Committee hearings on the IRS.

And what of the burden of proof? A clue to the bogus nature of the "reform" lies in the bill's command that Americans keep records and cooperate with the IRS during investigations. In other words, the IRS may have the nominal burden of proof, but you still must furnish the evidence it will use against you. No pleading the Fifth Amendment; that is for common criminals only. Moreover, to shift the burden to the government, a taxpayer will have to make a "reasonable" case that the IRS position is defective. In other words, the citizen has the burden of showing that the burden should be shifted! Some protection.

Even if there were a meaningful shift in the burden, it would be of no help to most taxpayers. "The problem," Pilla writes, "is that 97 percent of everything the IRS does involves no 'court proceeding.'" Most of the problems that citizens have with the IRS occur outside of the court. They involve, Pilla says, "its powers of lien, levy, and seizure." In other words, the shift in the burden is moot.

As the *Wall Street Journal* reported after Congress passed the IRS bill, "The change [shift of the burden] 'is not going to do much good' for most taxpayers battling the IRS, says N. Jerold Cohen, a lawyer at Sutherland Asbill in Atlanta and a former head of the American Bar Association tax section. 'It's a rare case that turns on the burden of proof.' Several other lawyers agree it will have mostly symbolic importance."[2]

I think what we have here is a public relations coup for the IRS and its allies in Congress. Don't expect any major breaks for the taxpayers.

But let us not be too cynical. There are other provisions of this bill that deserve attention. Ten years ago the Congress created the position of ombudsman, which was intended to be a liaison between taxpayers and the IRS. That was soon spotted for the sham it was, so in 1996, a new office was created: the taxpayer advocate. People saw through that too, and Congress in 1998 changed the office yet again. Now it is called the "national taxpayer advocate" and the position will be appointed by the treasury secretary instead of the IRS commissioner. Does anyone really expect such obvious window dressing to result in respect for the rights of American citizens?

But wait, there's more. The new law orders the IRS to evaluate its staff on the basis of its mission rather than on how much money or property it seizes from taxpayers. Despite congressional orders in the past, the IRS has continued to reward its people by their ability to bring in the bucks. That policy has been suspected of encouraging tax collectors to disregard the rights of taxpayers. The new law ostensibly solves that problem. But the mission of the IRS *is* to maximize the revenue harvest, so this is simply another ruse.

Bills of rights have never restrained the IRS. We shouldn't be surprised. It has a mandate to collect a trillion and a half dollars a year. You don't extract that kind of money by being Mr. Nice Guy. The IRS knows it. More important, the Congress knows it. It certainly wants the public-relations dividend of passing taxpayer-protection legislation, but it doesn't really want to do anything to reduce the fear and intimidation the American people experience at the thought of the IRS. The moment those things are reduced, people will do what they can to protect their incomes from the taxman. It's human nature. Tax revolts — even the quiet, private kind — are a constant feature of history. As long as there are taxmen and taxpayers, there will be tax avoidance. You'll sooner see things fall *up* than see truly voluntary compliance with the tax code, even if everyone understood it.

Revealingly, throughout the congressional deliberation on the latest taxpayer-protection law, there was great concern over what it would cost. Taxpayers' rights are fine as long as they aren't too expensive. In the eyes of the government, much of the cost comes not from spending on new equipment or personnel. It results from revenue forgone. In other words, money *not* extracted is treated as though it was spending. If the IRS stops collecting back taxes from an ex-spouse who had no idea the tax return had been incorrectly filed, that is counted as an expense chalked up to the new law.

This speaks volumes. The cost associated with government activity used to mean the cost *to* the taxpayers. Now it means the money the government might have taken from the taxpayers but didn't. Notice that whenever anyone suggests a tax cut, he is asked how he plans to pay for it. I guess we can say that part of the cost of the present tax code is the 80 percent of the gross domestic product that the government leaves in the taxpayers' pockets. Any tax increase can be heralded as a reduction in the cost of government. The people who think up these things are absolute geniuses.

This view of costs demonstrates that the purpose of the tax system is not to provide "service" to Americans. We are in no way the IRS's customers, as the commissioner likes to refer to us. We are its cash cows. Maybe they've decided that you get more milk with warm hands than cold.

There's no sense blaming the IRS for its disdainful attitude toward taxpayers. That would be like holding a bird responsible for eating worms: that's what it was born to do! It's not the agency's fault. The fault lies with Congress, which created the IRS and charged it with extracting so much from the hide of the American people. It can't do that while being gentle.

There is one way — and only one way — to respect taxpayers' rights: repeal all income taxes and the outrageous spending that requires them. "Taxpayers' rights" is actually a contradiction in terms, like vacation pay and free elections.

The torment that the IRS inflicts on individuals is horrific. People have lost their homes, businesses, and even their lives. But we must not let those terrible incidents make us forget the more general offense against the American people: the routine, day-to-day theft engaged in by government at all levels — most egregiously from income taxes.

Notes

[1] Daniel J. Pilla, "Revenue Neutral," *National Review*, June 1, 1998, p. 42. All Pilla quotes are from this article.

[2] Tom Herman, "Tax Notes," *Wall Street Journal Interactive Edition*, July 15, 1998 (http://interactive.wsj.com).

About the Author

Sheldon Richman is senior fellow at The Future of Freedom Foundation in Fairfax, Virginia, and the editor of *The Freeman*, published by The Foundation for Economic Education, Irvington-on-Hudson, New York. His first book, *Separating School & State: How to Liberate America's Families*, was published by The Future of Freedom Foundation in 1994. He formerly was senior editor at the Cato Institute and the Institute for Humane Studies at George Mason University.

Richman has written widely on a variety of topics, including education, population and the environment, taxation, federal disaster policy, international trade, the Second Amendment, and American history. His work has appeared in the *Washington Post*; *Wall Street Journal*; *USA Today*; *Washington Times*; *Chicago Tribune*; *Christian Science Monitor*; *San Francisco Chronicle*; *Detroit News*; *American Scholar*; *Journal of Economic Growth*; *Education Week*; *Regulation*; *The World and I*; *Insight*; *The Freeman*; *Reason*; and *Liberty*.

He is a contributor to *The Fortune Encyclopedia of Economics*.

Richman has appeared on CNN's *Crossfire* and *Both Sides* with Jesse Jackson; CNBC's *Business Insiders*; ABC's *This Week with David Brinkley*; the Montel Williams show; and radio programs across the United States.

He is formerly a newspaper reporter and magazine editor and was graduated from Temple University in his hometown, Philadelphia. He has three children, who are home-schooled.

About the Publisher

Founded in 1989, The Future of Freedom Foundation is a 501(c)(3), tax-exempt, educational foundation that presents an uncompromising moral, philosophical, and economic case for individual freedom, private property, and limited government.

The officers of The Foundation are: Jacob G. Hornberger (Fairfax, Virginia), president, and Richard M. Ebeling (Hillsdale, Michigan), vice president of academic affairs. There are eight members on The Foundation's board of trustees. *Freedom Daily* is published monthly by The Foundation. It consists of essays, book reviews, and quotes from freedom's greatest champions. Subscribers come from thirty countries. The price of a one-year subscription is $18 ($25 foreign). The Foundation also shares its ideas on liberty with others through lectures, speeches, seminars, and radio appearances.

The Foundation neither solicits nor accepts governmental funds. Operations are financed through subscription revenues and donations, which are invited in any amount. Please write us for additional information. We hope you will join us in this important work.

The Future of Freedom Foundation
11350 Random Hills Road, Suite 800
Fairfax, Virginia 22030
(703) 934-6101
Fax (703) 352-8678
http://www.fff.org

Index